# THE BRONTËS

*and their world*

The three Brontë sisters, painted by Branwell

# THE BRONTËS

*and their world*

BY PHYLLIS BENTLEY

A STUDIO BOOK

THE VIKING PRESS · NEW YORK

Copyright © 1969 Phyllis Bentley & Thames and Hudson Ltd
All rights reserved

Published in 1969 by the Viking Press, Inc., 625 Madison Avenue, New York, N.Y. 10022

Library of Congress catalog card number: 69-17972

SBN. 670–19235–X

Second Printing September 1970

Printed in Great Britain by Jarrold and Sons Ltd, Norwich, England

The Mountains of Mourne, visible from the cottage where Patrick Brontë was born

ON ST PATRICK'S DAY, that is 17 March, in the year 1777, their eldest child, a son, was born to Hugh and Eleanor Brunty in their whitewashed cabin in the parish of Drumballyroney, Emdale, County Down, Northern Ireland. The child, the first of ten, was christened Patrick.

Emdale is a remote valley lying between two tiny towns (Roughbrickland and *Emdale* Rathfriland) in the heart of a series of gently rolling hills. The countryside is quiet, lonely, serene, sheltered. Fields of golden oats alternate with green, very green grass sprinkled with branching thistles; the hedges are thick with fuchsia and honeysuckle; a few sheep browse on the slopes; the mild, somehow rather wistful and melancholy Irish air blows softly over all. Between the curves of the hills, in the distance, tower romantically the Mountains of Mourne, dark blue and aquiline, whose further slopes, as we know from the song, roll down to the sea.

5

Until recently the two-roomed Brunty cabin stood decaying in more or less its original shape, its thatched roof partly fallen, its walls breaking down. But in 1956 the Irish Tourist Board gathered up its tumbled stones, protected the site by a wall and honoured it by a plaque stating that this was the birthplace of the father of the Brontës.

Hugh Brunty was a poor peasant farmer of Northern Irish, possibly originally Scottish, extraction, and certainly Protestant in religion; his wife Eleanor, sometimes called Alice, was certainly from the south of Ireland and possibly Catholic in religion. The children were, however, brought up Protestant.

When I was in Emdale in 1932, the children of the valley went about barefooted, and it is reasonable to assume that a hundred and fifty years earlier Patrick Brunty did the same. He was a boy of commanding presence, however, tall, with dark red hair and pale blue eyes, vigorous in body and decidedly strong in mind.

The Reverend John Wesley, leader of the Methodist Society

Cottage in the parish of Drumballyroney, County Down, where Patrick Brontë was born, 1777
'A cottage on the green;
. . . The walls were white,
The thatch was neat,
The window bright.'
(Patrick Brontë, *Cottage Poems*)

6

Parish Church School at Drumballyroney, where Patrick Brontë taught from 1789 to 1802

He taught himself to read from the three or four books which his practically illiterate parents chanced to own, and though he was first apprenticed to a blacksmith, and then as linen weaver and draper, by the time he was sixteen he was already teaching in the Presbyterian school in the neighbouring village of Glascar, and then in the Parish Church School of Drumballyroney. Presently the widowed vicar of near-by Drumgooland, the Rev. Thomas Tighe, invited him to become tutor to his two young sons. It is to be noted that Mr Tighe was a friend of John Wesley, who stayed with him during his preaching tours. To provide for the service of God a young preacher of ability would be thoroughly in line with Wesley's, and thus with Tighe's, views. Mr Tighe coached Patrick, perhaps lent him a little money, set him on the way to university.

St John's College, Cambridge, in 1819. Patrick Brontë became a sizar here in 1802 and obtained his B A degree in 1806

In 1802, at the age of twenty-five, Patrick entered St John's College, Cambridge, as a sizar, that is, as a student receiving financial assistance from his college on the grounds of poverty. While in college he eked out his resources by coaching other students, and by receiving some assistance from a charitable group of rich fellow-students. He made no debts, and was even able to send money home to his mother from time to time.

The immense social and psychological distance which Patrick had travelled, in the snobbish early nineteenth century, from a whitewashed cabin in Emdale to Cambridge University, is the measure of his mental capacity and robust determination. His new status appears, perhaps not altogether creditably, in his change of name at this point. Whether the St John's Registrar was confused between Branty, Brunty and Brontë by the new student's Irish accent, or whether Patrick took advantage of this confusion, we shall never know, but from this time Patrick becomes first Bronte, then Bronté and finally Brontë. It is not irrelevant

Woodhouse Grove School, Apperley Bridge, near Bradford, 1812. Mr Brontë examined the boys in religious instruction, and met Maria Branwell here

to either hypothesis that the great Lord Nelson had been made Duke of Brontë in 1799, and we note that more than forty years later, after the publication of *Jane Eyre*, it was rumoured about London that the Brontës 'are of the Nelson family'. But let us give Patrick the benefit of the doubt. Once he had taken his degree in the name of Brontë, of course he had to stick to it.

*West Riding*

Patrick took his degree in 1806, was ordained, held curacies in Wethersfield (Essex) and Wellington (Shropshire), and finally came to the West Riding of Yorkshire in 1809, being recommended to a vicar there by William Morgan, a fellow curate at Wellington, who like Patrick had Wesleyan friends and patrons. In 1811 Patrick became minister at Hartshead, a village not far from Brighouse. William Morgan was engaged to Miss Jane Fennell, daughter of the principal of a school for the sons of Wesleyan ministers at Woodhouse Grove, Apperley Bridge, not far from Bradford. Morgan naturally took Patrick with him to visit at the Fennells', and Patrick became examiner to the pupils in theology. Staying

(Above left) Maria Branwell as a girl in 1799

(Left) Guiseley Parish Church, where Patrick Brontë and Maria Branwell were married on 29 December 1812

(Above) Penzance, Cornwall, 1825. Maria Branwell lived here with her family till she was nearly thirty

with the Fennells at this time was one of their cousins from Penzance (Cornwall), the small, neat, well-educated, highly intelligent, recently orphaned Miss Maria Branwell. Patrick Brontë and Maria Branwell fell in love, and there was a double wedding – Fennell–Morgan, Branwell–Brontë – in December 1812.

Though much enlarged and differently organized, the school still stands there, nor has the parlour where Mr Brontë, as we must call him now that he is a clergyman of the Church of England, conducted his courtship, been structurally altered.

If Mr Brontë had a strong and an unusual history, Mrs Brontë, born in 1783, was equally interesting in a different way. Her father was a prosperous merchant and a member of the Town Council in Penzance. Letters written by Maria to Patrick during their courtship reveal her as a most charming, sympathetic, affectionate girl, well able to express herself in writing and not lacking in a gentle

*Maria Branwell*

11

humour. It must be remembered that at this time Mr Brontë was a lively, good-looking, talkative fellow, with Irish blarney no doubt in his tongue, but a good preacher, sincerely religious, and the author of a volume, *Cottage Poems*, which he had just published locally, in Halifax. Maria addresses him once as 'my own saucy Pat', and we discern between her modest, playful lines that the cause of the epithet was a stolen kiss. It was during this period of courtship that Maria wrote, 'for insertion in one of the periodical publications', an essay entitled 'On the Advantages of Poverty in Religious Concerns'. Pious and sincere, entirely correct in the style of the time, the essay contains nothing original or striking and did not achieve, perhaps did not seriously attempt, publication.

*Patrick's writing*   But it has its importance. So have Mr Brontë's productions. He published in all two volumes of poems, two prose tales, three pamphlets and two sermons, besides several articles and poems in local newspapers. His poetry (*Cottage Poems*, 1811, and *The Rural Minstrel*, 1813) is the merest verse, honest, well meaning, but pompous and boring. *The Cottage in the Wood*, 1815, is a religious tale, on Sunday-school prize level, of a virtuous peasant girl who converts the rake who

Title-pages of *Cottage Poems* and *The Cottage in the Wood* by the Rev. Patrick Brontë

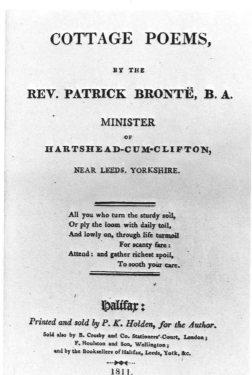

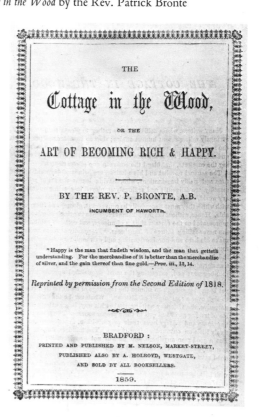

Maria Branwell, Mrs Brontë. 'At
once sad and sweet, to find that mind
of a truly fine, pure and elevated order.'
(Charlotte, on reading her mother's
letters in 1850)

pursues her, into Christian marriage. It has little dialogue and is inconceivably
dull. *The Maid of Killarney, or Albion and Flora*, was printed in 1818, anonymously,
in London. This is the tale of a young Englishman meeting and marrying an
Irish girl, in Ireland; it includes discussions on the Duke of Wellington, Catholic
Emancipation, the British and Foreign Bible Society, and other topics of the day,
also a lively description of an Irish wake and a night attack by that Irish secret
society of the day, the eviction-maddened Whiteboys. We shall meet the name
of Albion again later, employed by the next Brontë generation, and one of the
phrases: 'To the finest fibre of my nature, sir!' is echoed in *Jane Eyre*.

But apart from these slender connections, the fact that Mr Brontë and his wife
both had literary aspirations, and that Mr Brontë achieved publication, was of
very real significance in their children's lives. From their earliest days, the children
saw printed books with their papa's name on the title-page, not only in their own
home but actually displayed in shop windows. No wonder that their thoughts
were turned towards writing and that, as Charlotte tells us, 'the highest stimulus,
as well as the liveliest pleasure we had known from childhood upwards, lay in
attempts at literary composition'.

Mr and Mrs Brontë were both Celtic in origin, both sincerely religious with a
favourable inclination towards the reforming zeal of Wesley; both were well

Thornton Vicarage. The birthplace of Charlotte, Patrick Branwell, Emily Jane and Anne Brontë

Rev. Patrick Brontë in 1825, five years after his arrival in Haworth

The Old Bell Chapel, Thornton

Interior of the Old Bell Chapel

Haworth Parsonage from the graveyard as it was in the Brontës' time. The figure by the side of the house may be that of Charlotte

informed on current affairs; both were well read and fond of reading; both inclined to 'literary composition'; both were, in Yorkshire, a long way from their families and native homes. Some of these qualities they bequeathed to their children; all tended to make a special mental climate in their children's lives.

At the time of his marriage Mr Brontë was still minister at Hartshead, and his eldest two children were born there, Maria in 1813, Elizabeth in 1815. That year he moved towards the north-west, exchanging the living of Hartshead for that of Thornton, with the Rev. Thomas Atkinson, who desired the move in order to be nearer to the lady he was courting. The Brontës made good friends in Thornton, some of whom were godparents to their famous children who were born there: Charlotte in 1816, Patrick Branwell, the only son, in 1817, Emily Jane in 1818, and Anne in 1820. In 1820 Mr Brontë was appointed incumbent of Haworth, and moved his family to Haworth Parsonage, going, again, north-west to do so. Unfortunately, in the autumn of 1821, poor young Mrs Brontë, after bearing six children in seven years, died of cancer. Mr Brontë made two attempts to remarry, proposing to a lady in Thornton and to an early love in

*Family*

15

16

(Left) Old Haworth Church, built before 1500. Except for the old tower, the church was rebuilt, on its former site, in 1879

(Left below) Old Haworth Church: interior

Elizabeth Branwell, sister of Mrs Brontë

Wethersfield whom he had jilted, but both were unsuccessful. Mrs Brontë's sister, Miss Elizabeth Branwell, who had come to Haworth during Maria's illness, agreed to return and remain to superintend the housekeeping of Haworth Parsonage and care for her sister's motherless children. From then onwards Haworth remained the Brontës' home.

Miss Elizabeth Branwell, though a gentlewoman, intelligent, well informed, *Aunt Branwell* conversationally apt and skilled in needlework, had not the loving, warm-hearted, tender nature of her sister. She kept the Parsonage to regular, orderly ways and brought up the children well, but it is noticeable that in all the more than four hundred Brontë letters still available, she is never referred to with affection. The children respected her rule but did not love her; they called her *Aunt*, never *Auntie* or *Aunt Bessie*. They also laughed a little at her false front of auburn curls, her silk dresses, and the pattens (wooden over-shoes) she wore in the house, and they were tired of hearing her unfavourable comparisons of Haworth with Penzance. For indeed Haworth was a sore trial to Miss Branwell. Cornwall has

17

a much milder, drier climate than the bleak and windy West Riding. Palm trees grow out of doors in Penzance, the sun shines and the sea is blue. In Penzance Miss Branwell had friends and intellectual equals, tea-parties and social calls; Haworth lacked all these.

To move north-west in the West Riding of Yorkshire is to move further into the Pennine Chain, the range of mountains which runs due north and south down the middle of England, from the Scottish border to the Peak in Derbyshire. The village of Haworth stands on an outlying spur of this chain. The name is derived, according to some authorities, from Saxon words meaning *high farm*; according to others, from Norse words indicating a high mound and the River Worth. The latter derivation seems perhaps more probable, for Haworth certainly does stretch up from the foot to the summit of a long high mound; in the valley at its foot on one side flows the River Worth, in the valley on its other side flows, rather nearer, a tributary of this river. The nearest town is Keighley, lying four miles down the Worth Valley, in the other direction a moorland road leads eventually to Hebden Bridge, a little town lying in the Calder valley eight miles away, and thence to Halifax, a sizable town some seven miles further down the same Calder Dale. But these are Pennine miles; the roads have steep gradients, and are wild and windy, exposed to every kind of weather. In the Brontës' days there was no railway from Haworth, no bus service; if one wanted to leave the village one walked, or rode if one could afford a horse, or hired a gig or a covered carrier's cart.

Readers from the south of England and more distant places have said that they never understood the Brontës' writings until they had seen Haworth. One enters the village in the valley, turns sharply right, crosses a bridge, climbs steeply upwards; at the top of this slope one turns right again and finds oneself confronted with an even longer, steeper slope – a narrow cobbled road, lined on each side by smallish, darkish stone houses. They are built of millstone grit, the hard dark rock on which Haworth stands. Almost at the top, one passes the Black Bull inn on the left, turns to the left and comes to Haworth Church, dedicated to St Michael and All Angels. This is not the church in which the Brontës worshipped, for it was rebuilt in 1879, but its site is the same. Passing along its side up the narrow cobbled lane, observing the graveyard with its many gravestones sweeping up to the wall of the little Parsonage garden, one comes to Haworth Parsonage itself. This was added to in the 1860s, but the original plain, two-storeyed early Georgian building, gazing eastward over graveyard and church to distant hills, remains, nowadays as a museum.

Behind the Parsonage a pathway through fields leads to the moors. Sombre, sweeping slopes of black rock, rough pale grass and tough heather – the latter magnificently purple in August and September, dark brown at all other periods of the year – are scoured by strong Atlantic winds which drive clouds turbulently

19

Haworth Village. 'A populous manufacturing village, containing, by the census of 1821, 4668 inhabitants.' (*Pigot's Yorkshire Directory of 1828*)

Haworth Moor ▶

RAWFOLDS MILL

Rawfolds Mill. Charlotte combined with this certain features of Hunsworth, the mill of her friends the Taylors, to make Hollows Mill and Cottage in *Shirley*

across the grey sky. Innumerable 'becks', as Yorkshire people call their small streams, throw themselves fiercely down their narrow rocky beds, giving the landscape that leaping thread of white and sound of tumbling water, so dear to native eyes and ears. Rain is frequent, mist is frequent, in winter snow is frequent, so that tall posts stand at the side to guide the traveller and keep him to the path. The West Riding moorland is not picturesque, probably not romantically beautiful to a stranger's eye, certainly not pretty, but untamed by the hand of man, it has a vigour sometimes (under sunny skies) cheerfully robust, sometimes grimly sullen, which encourages these feelings in Yorkshire hearts. Even the sheep, browsing solitary here and there, look up startled and unfriendly, and seem to share the prevailing independence and reserve.

The little Brontës roamed these moors and loved them dearly – especially Emily. 'My sister Emily', wrote Charlotte later, 'loved the moors. . . . They were far more to her than a mere spectacle; they were what she lived in and by, as much as the wild birds, their tenants, or the heather, their produce. . . . She found in the bleak solitude many and dear delights; and not the least and best loved was – liberty.'

The Haworth background influenced the Brontës' lives in another way, which they perhaps did not realize. Not fertile agricultural country – oats were the only possible grain and they grew but scantily – and not affording rich pasture for cows, but lavishly provided with water devoid of lime and grass and heather suitable for the food of sheep, the West Riding had the wool and water necessary for the textile industry, and had accordingly been engaged in the domestic manufacture and market of wool cloth for some six centuries. In the early decades of the nineteenth century, machines for textile processes were introduced, which were run first by water-power and then by steam. The workers resisted the coming of the machines, and in 1812 there were riots in Hartshead, where Mr Brontë was at that time minister. But as usual technological improvements won the day. These developments gathered the textile workers from their cottages in the upper folds of the hills to mills built down by the larger streams, first to secure the water-power, then for easy access by the coal necessary for steam, and to cluster labour economically round one steam-engine. A new social stratum, of millowners, thus arose, a group new to English society, a good deal richer than the local clergy, but much less well educated. These manufacturers, as they now called themselves, desired gentry education for their children, and small local schools, tutors and governesses, came increasingly into demand.

Textile workers who became Luddites when their hand-labour was superseded by 'frames'

23

Rev. Carus Wilson. 'A wealthy clergyman . . . willing to sacrifice everything but power.' (Mrs Gaskell, *Life*) 'A black pillar! The straight, narrow, sable-clad shape standing erect on the rug.' (Charlotte of the Rev. Mr Brocklehurst, *Jane Eyre*)

Thus the Brontës' world was formed by a decidedly unusual combination of elements. Their heredity was Celtic – a character usually eloquent, expressive, extravert. Their environment was Yorkshire – amongst a people realistic, practical, reserved, greatly disliking any too great revelation of feeling. The Brontë children could speak and write both Irish and Yorkshire forms of speech, and in her teens Charlotte still had an Irish accent. These differing influences of course inhabited and perhaps divided their minds, and we can see their varied occurrence in the six children. Branwell talkative, volatile, always on show; Emily utterly reserved, strong in her own private intention; Anne, most like her mother perhaps, sweetly pious and resigned; Charlotte always in battle between her strong morality and her equally strong sexual intimations. Of Elizabeth we know too little to speak. Maria appears to have been completely serene in spirit, but her mental division shows in her outward untidiness, if we are to accept her portrait as Helen Burns in *Jane Eyre*. Added to these conflicting elements in the Brontës was their nearness to the moorland, a bleak grandeur which stripped their taste to the austere and nourished their love of independence. They inherited a love of books, their family life encouraged this love, and it was encouraged the more by their loneliness. For in their immediate world they had no young relatives, nobody with whom to play on equal terms. William Morgan's wife, their mother's cousin, died soon after her marriage; after that Aunt Branwell was their only relative in Yorkshire.

*Clergy
Daughters'
School*

To Mr Brontë, who had six children to educate on an income of £200 a year

The Clergy Daughters' School

and a rent-free house, the foundation of the Clergy Daughters' School at Cowan Bridge, on the borders of Lancashire and Westmorland, by the Rev. William Carus Wilson, must have appeared a godsend. Mr Wilson was an earnest, wealthy landowner of good intentions, devoutly religious in the Evangelical belief, who aimed to provide board and education for the daughters of the clergy for a fee of £14 a year, the remaining sums necessary being provided by charitable subscriptions. The school, founded in January 1824 in a cottage and bobbin-mill adapted to his purpose, held by July of that year, when Mr Brontë took there his eldest two daughters, Maria (aged eleven) and Elizabeth (aged nine), twenty-nine pupils, a number which rapidly increased. Mr Brontë stayed the night and ate with the pupils, and returned in August and November respectively with his next two daughters, Charlotte and Emily.

The frightful pictures of Cowan Bridge and Mr Carus Wilson, drawn as Lowood and Mr Brocklehurst by Charlotte in *Jane Eyre*, and confirmed in Mrs Gaskell's *Life of Charlotte Brontë*, aroused immense controversy, indignant relatives on both sides plunging fiercely into the fray. But with every respect for Mr Carus Wilson's motives, anyone who has read one of his little *Children's Friend* magazines or his stories for children, cannot but agree with a shudder that his conception of the right kind of tuition for children was totally and most horribly wrong. His writings abound in deathbed stories of little children. One little boy of three and a half, asked whether he would choose death or life, replies:

25

'Death for me. I am fonder of death.' Mr Wilson's fictitious children continually pray, in terms nauseating to a modern ear; a 'naughty child, who screamed and cried,' is suddenly struck dead by God, and goes, of course, to hell! Another of these naughty little beings, inquiring plaintively: 'Why do they whip us, if they love us?' is told that they are whipped in order to save their souls. Mr Wilson was, indeed, so utterly mistaken about human nature that he not only thought gruesome tales of death and hell suitable reading for young children and frequent punishment a proper mode of upbringing, he also believed that perpetual reminders to the older girls of their dependent position would induce in them a proper humility. In Charlotte's proud soul, on the contrary, his methods created a passionate and lasting resentment.

Physically, too, the severe régime of the school was unsuited to the delicate little Brontës, who in any case had only just recovered from measles and whooping cough. Even the best of boarding-schools is not as comfortable as home. Cowan Bridge was cold, especially when 'the great girls', as Charlotte tells us, clustered round the fire, shutting out its warmth from those of smaller stature. The walk over the hill on Sunday to Mr Wilson's church at Tunstall was in winter an agony; snow slopped into the girls' shoes and their gloveless hands froze; they remained in the unwarmed church, with wet feet, all day. The food at the school was poor, badly bought and badly cooked; the little Brontës often could not eat it.

So it came about that gentle Maria Brontë developed tuberculosis, and in February 1825 was sent home ill. She died on 6 May. Elizabeth Brontë was by this time also ill with tuberculosis, and came home on 31 May. Fortunately Mr Brontë took alarm at this, went off next day to Cowan Bridge, found that Charlotte and Emily had been sent to Mr Wilson's seaside residence at Silverdale, and brought them home to Haworth. Elizabeth died on 15 June.

What Charlotte thought about all this can be read in *Jane Eyre*. Branwell too was deeply affected by Maria's death, as can be seen in his poems, *Misery II*, *Harriet*, *Caroline* and others.

From 1825 to 1831 the remaining Brontës – Papa, Charlotte, Branwell, Emily, Anne – and their aunt Miss Branwell, lived together in Haworth Parsonage. Mr Brontë was the conscientious and active priest of a far-flung parish, who sat on local committees and strove vigorously for the spiritual and physical welfare of Haworth. In the intervals of his parochial commitments he taught Branwell, whom he instructed in Greek and Latin as well as in ordinary English subjects. Unfortunately, the brilliant lad, after a few useless months at a not very good local establishment, was never sent to school, for Mr Brontë could not have afforded to pay for schooling for his son comparable to that which his father, a BA Cantab. after all, could give him. Miss Branwell gave the girls lessons in her bedroom, and also taught them to be good housewives and needle-women.

Tunstall Church. The Rev. Carus Wilson's church, which the Cowan Bridge pupils attended every Sunday

One other person of importance in the family life had been added to the household. In the kitchen was now the middle-aged widow, Tabitha Aykroyd, Tabby as they called her. Tabby cooked and cleaned and ruled the children with a rough though loving hand. Fiercely honest and decent, a thorough Yorkshire-woman, who spoke strong Yorkshire dialect and had all the independence and blunt speech of her kind, she was a faithful servant to the Brontës for thirty years. Later she was joined, at the age of ten, by one of the Sexton's many children, Martha Brown, who was still at the Parsonage in 1861.

These six years when they were all at home together were an extremely important formative period in the young Brontës' lives. Lacking playmates, they learned to wish for none. They roamed the moors. They cherished pets. Emily's famous mastiff, Keeper, and Anne's silky spaniel, Flossy, are later examples in a long series of dogs, cats, birds. Ailing or damaged birds and animals found in the

27

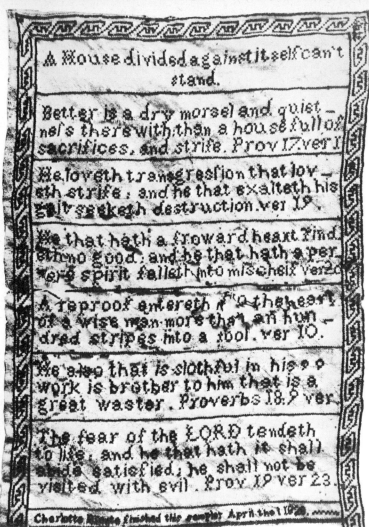

A House divided against itself can't
stand.

Better is a dry morsel and quiet_
ness therewith, than a house full of
sacrifices, and strife. Prov 17 ver 1

He loveth transgression that lov_
eth strife; and he that exalteth his
gate seeketh destruction. ver 19

He that hath a froward heart find_
eth no good; and he that hath a per_
verse spirit falleth into mischeif ver 20

A reproof entereth more into the heart
of a wise man more than an hun_
dred stripes into a fool. ver 10.

He also that is slothful in his
work is brother to him that is a
great waster. Proverbs 18 9 ver

The fear of the LORD tendeth
to life; and he that hath it shall
abide satisfied; he shall not be
visited with evil. Prov 19 ver 23.

Charlotte Brontë finished this sampler April the 1 1829.

Sampler by Charlotte Brontë

A page from 'The History of the Year
1829' by Charlotte Brontë

Double page of 'The
History of the Young
Men' (actual size),
written by Charlotte
*c.* 1825

28

Church drawn by Anne Brontë

Map of the Great Glass Town Confederacy, drawn by Branwell

parish were often brought to the Brontës, who nursed them tenderly back to health. Any persons who showed a harsh or careless attitude towards the animal world earned the Brontës' contempt.

*Childhood writings*

But the important point is that during these six years they began to create, to invent, and to write their inventions down in fictitious form. We have accounts from Charlotte and Branwell of how this story-making began.

One night in June 1826, a year after the death of his eldest daughters, Mr Brontë brought home from Leeds for Branwell a box of wooden soldiers, with other gifts, including a model village, for the three girls. The children were asleep, so he laid the soldiers beside the boy's bed. Next morning Branwell came to the girls' door with the soldiers.

> Emily and I jumped out of bed, and I snatched up one and exclaimed: 'This is the Duke of Wellington! This shall be the Duke!' Emily likewise took up a soldier, a grave-looking fellow, and said he should be hers; we called him Gravey. When Anne came downstairs (Anne slept in Aunt's room), she also chose one, a queer-looking thing.

They called him 'Waiting-Boy'. Branwell's choice was grandiloquently named Buonaparte. These soldiers became the characters in endless tales of wars and battles founded on the Napoleonic campaigns, then so recent and so familiar in England. 'The Young Men', as they were called, or sometimes 'The Twelves', presently developed other names and other characteristics and other adventures. Each of the original soldiers had at first a kingdom of his own – Parrysland, Sneachisland, and so on, of which Branwell drew a map; eventually all this invention settled into a whole imaginary world, called the 'Great Glass Town Confederacy', which had publishers and authors, inns, magazines, generals, artists, heroes, rogues, just like the real world. Over Great Glass Town presided the Four Genii, whose names are given as Tallii, Brannii, Emmii and Annii.

Concrete images of Great Glass Town were perhaps derived from the rather grandiose Biblical pictures of John Martin, fashionable artist of the Annuals so popular in the 1820s. Four engravings of Martin's hung in the Parsonage, including *Belshazzar's Feast*, by which the architectural features of this imaginary capital city were most probably inspired. Great Glass Town personages were similarly copied, stroke by stroke, from Annuals illustrations.

Other plays were invented from time to time; Charlotte gives us a vivid picture of how the four children, sitting round the kitchen fire one stormy winter's night, forbidden a candle by the economical Tabby, began *The Islanders* play by each choosing an island and peopling it with their favourite celebrities.

Great Glass Town, however, remained the chief employment of their agile brains. In January 1829 Branwell invented *The Young Men's Magazine*. Charlotte

John Martin's *Belshazzar's Feast*. Martin's pictures obviously inspired Great Glass Town's architecture

contributed to it and soon took it over. Into this they poured Glass Town essays, Glass Town histories, Glass Town songs. After 1830 the Brontës showed their increasing sophistication by renaming Glass Town as Verreopolis (from the French for glass, obviously, with a classic termination) and this soon became Verdopolis.

During the early years of this extraordinary creation the main figure shifted from the imaginary Duke of Wellington to his imaginary son, Arthur August Adrian Wellesley, Marquess of Douro. An early tale about Wellesley is entitled *Albion and Marina*, Wellesley being depicted as Albion. Charlotte and Branwell, deciding that Douro should have a kingdom of his own, invented the kingdom of Angria, and Arthur became Duke of Zamorna and King of Angria. Charlotte conducted the romances of Angria, giving Zamorna two wives and several mistresses – her characterization of these is superb. Branwell conducted the parliaments and wars of Angria, inventing as Zamorna's adversary the wicked pirate, Rogue.

31

(Right) Title-pages of one of the
'Young Men's Magazine' series,
edited by Charlotte, and of 'Letters
from an Englishman' by Branwell

The Duke of Wellington,
Charlotte and Branwell's great hero,
in whom originated all the
Angrian stories

Emily and Anne presently left Angria and invented a kingdom of their own, Gondal, which had a climate like that of Haworth and a wild, fierce queen.

Emily continued Gondal, we gather, all her life. There are no prose Gondal works by Emily and Anne in existence – it may be that Charlotte destroyed them after her sisters' deaths, we do not know. But references to Gondal characters occur in birthday notes written between Emily and Anne as late as 1845, and many of Emily's poems are Gondal in subject. Charlotte bade a formal farewell to Angria in writing, when she was twenty-three. Branwell's Angrian writings appear to cease in 1839, when he was twenty-two. There still exists, however, a mass of these childhood writings, rather greater in wordage than the whole of the Brontës' published works.

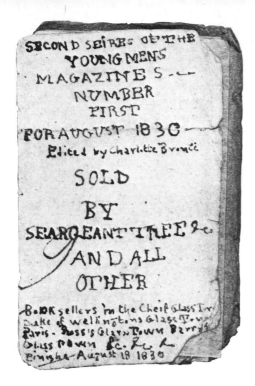

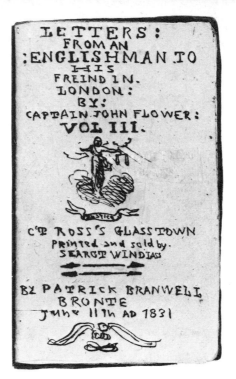

The fact which gives all this vast amount of writing an almost eerie fascination is that it was mostly written in tiny hand-printing on tiny folded sheets of paper, often only about 2 inches by 1½ inches (5 cm. by 4 cm.) in size. These tiny leaves are stitched neatly together to form delicious little books, given elaborate title-pages and backed with sugar-bag or other shop wrapping-paper. (Inside the back of one of these can be read the words: *Purified Epsom Salts. J. West, Chemist and Druggist. Keighley.*) Why the Brontës employed such tiny scraps of paper is an interesting question. Originally it doubtless sprang from a lack of larger material and a lack of pocket-money with which to buy any; but presently the desire for secrecy probably crept in, for even when the leaves grew larger, the hand-printing remains minute. There is in the Parsonage Museum an exercise book of normal size, inscribed: 'All that is written in this book must be in a good, plain and legible hand. P.B.' This seems to imply that Mr Brontë had accidentally caught sight of some of the tiny hand-printing, and disapproved, as indeed any parent might disapprove, of such a threat to his children's eyesight. The exercise book is empty.

These childhood writings about what Charlotte calls 'the world below' are of course daydreams in the Freudian sense, expressing suppressed desires. Charlotte's passionate interest in sex, Branwell's passionate rebellion, Emily's passionate love of freedom – the deepest and most significant part of their lives – are displayed before us and shed a rather lurid light on later occurrences. We see that Branwell is not nearly such a good prose writer as Charlotte. His style is grandiose and pompous, he is too fond of boring detail, put in to show that he knows it; to put it bluntly, he is conceited, and it is Charlotte who clothes Branwell's character of Rogue the pirate in flesh and blood. We also see Charlotte teasing her brother – who appears in the Angrian story sometimes as Patrick Benjamin Wiggins, a poet – for his boastful lying. Wiggins, walking in the exodus from Verdopolis to Angria, in describing his journey exaggerates his mileage from twenty to sixty miles a day; he enters an inn and emerges boasting of the beef and beer he has consumed, when in fact his meal was tea and bread and butter. This habit of excited exaggeration, lovingly joked about by an admiring sister, entertaining enough in childhood, reappears tragically in later life.

One set of Yorkshire verses, contained in a Verdopolitan story by Charlotte, *The Foundling*, when she is referring to some odd little personages obviously, by their physical structure, intended to be members of Emily's model village, might well give us the clue to Emily if we could relate it to reality. At Cowan Bridge Emily, according to the headmistress, was 'a darling child . . . quite the pet nursling of the school'. Was the incident described in these verses a real one, a traumatic experience which drove this darling Emily into the strange reserve which is all we know of her? We cannot tell.

'Eamala' is of course Yorkshire for 'Emily'.

> *Eamala is a great bellaring bull,*
> *Shoo swilled and swilled till shoo drank her full;*
> *Then shoo rolled abaat*
> *Wi' a screaam an' shaat*
> *And aat of her pocket a knoife did pull.*
>
> *An' wi' that knife shood' a cutt her throit*
> *If I hadn't gean her a strait waist-coit . . .*

Eventually Eamala sleeps till 'all the gooid liquor wor gooan fro her head.'

One important result, perhaps indeed two, accrued from this prodigious amount of writing. When the young Brontës at length began to write of real life they were not amateurs, but experienced craftsmen, thoroughly familiar with the handling of plot and characterization. But artistic creation of any kind is extremely exhausting. Did the young Brontës wear themselves out by this lush invention, this continual story-telling?

In 1831 a change came into their lives.

*Roe Head*    The young Brontës' contacts with the outer world always occurred in the sphere of education. In the autumn of 1830 Mr Brontë had a very severe attack of congestion of the lungs, from which he almost did not recover, and this

Roe Head, Miss Wooler's school. Drawn by Anne Brontë. 'A cheerful, roomy, country house.' (Mrs Gaskell, *Life*)

awakened, or at any rate confirmed, his anxiety about his children's future. What would happen to his four children, aged from fourteen downwards, if he died? They would be left without home, for the next incumbent of Haworth would at once occupy the Parsonage, and without resources, for he had nothing to leave to them. They must accordingly be taught to earn their living. A school had just been started at Roe Head in Mirfield, only about twenty miles away, within the West Riding, by a Miss Margaret Wooler, and Charlotte's godparents, the Rev. Thomas Atkinson (he with whom Mr Brontë had once exchanged parishes) and his wife, offered to pay Charlotte's fees there. Charlotte was accordingly entered as a pupil at Roe Head, and journeyed there in the Haworth covered cart in January 1831.

Ellen Nussey, drawn by Charlotte. 'When I first saw Ellen I did not care for her. . . . She is without romance . . . but she is good; she is true; she is faithful, and I love her.' (Charlotte, *Letter*)

Miss Margaret Wooler was a very unusual woman. Not quite forty in 1831, she was 'short and stout, but graceful in her movements, very fluent in conversation and with a very sweet voice. . . . She wore white, well-fitting dresses, embroidered. Her long hair plaited, formed a coronet, and long large ringlets fell from her head to shoulders. She was not pretty or handsome, but her quiet dignity made her presence imposing.' So said one of her pupils. She was thoroughly well read, knew French and Italian, and indeed read a portion of the Bible in Italian every day. The three of her sisters who formed her staff were not as well loved, but they were not feared or hated. Roe Head was a fine large eighteenth-century house, well situated on a rising slope, with large grounds, and the Roe Head régime was admirably suited to growing girls. The food was good and plentiful, the house well warmed; the girls had plenty of sleep, fresh air and exercise; the teaching was clear and worthy of respect; the discipline though firm was mild. Any breach of rules, unladylike manners or incorrect grammar, was punished by a black ribbon worn Garter-style by the offending pupil; on the other hand, due fulfilment of duties entitled the pupil to wear a silver medal. When weather made outdoor exercise impossible, Miss Wooler joined her pupils in their hour of relaxation,

Rydings, Birstall Ellen Nussey's home. Branwell called it 'Paradise!'

and paced slowly up and down the room, conversing. The girls hung around her, delighted to listen to her and to be part of the group. This cultured milieu must have suited Charlotte well, once she had grown used to it, in spite of her home, sickness, and it softened a character formed by the rigours of Haworth.

Charlotte made two great friends among her ten schoolmates at Roe Head. It is a tribute to her that Ellen Nussey and Mary Taylor differed so markedly in appearance, nature and social background.

To Ellen Nussey we owe a debt of eternal gratitude, for she kept every letter *Ellen Nussey* Charlotte wrote to her. These began in the Spring holidays in May 1831 and continued till Charlotte's death, so that more than four hundred of the precious documents remain available. Ellen's family was 'county', Conservative and Church of England. Her great-uncle, and four subsequent members, had been Court physicians; others were important local magistrates. Though her immediate family was in uncomfortable financial circumstances since the recent death of her father, rich relatives had come to their aid, and Ellen now lived in a large old turret-roofed house called 'Rydings', with large grounds, fine chestnut trees, and a rookery, in Birstall, a village some ten miles from Roe Head. She had numerous

Stained-glass
window from the
Red House,
Gomersal, the
home of the
Taylors

brothers and sisters, with whose characters and vicissitudes Charlotte became
thoroughly familiar. Ellen was sincerely religious, a gentlewoman by birth and
upbringing, pleasant-looking with a 'quiet fair face' but not beautiful, reasonably
intelligent but not outstandingly clever, not poetical or romantic but thoroughly
honest, altogether a nice good girl but one would have thought rather dull.
Charlotte, writing about her later, admits all this but says that she and Ellen
'suited'. The deeper level of Charlotte's nature, however, 'the world below', was
never hinted at to Ellen, and Charlotte did not confess the authorship of her
novels to this friend until growing publicity made the admission inevitable.

*Mary Taylor*    Mary Taylor was of an entirely different type. True, her family had been
established in the West Riding since 1379, and lived in a charming 1660 house,
the Red House, Gomersal, so called because unlike the mostly stone-built houses
of the area it was and still is of brick. But far from being 'county', Conservative,
or Anglican, the Taylors were violently Radical and Dissenting. Mary's father
was a wool cloth manufacturer, who had been severely hit by the cessation of the
Napoleonic Wars, when his manufacture of cloth for the army had come to a
sudden stop. He continued in business, however, determined to pay his debts.

Current events, bread shortages
and riots, which the Taylors
probably discussed

Mr Taylor was a thorough dialect-speaking Yorkshireman, but also a man who had travelled much in Europe, spoke French well, read French books and newspapers regularly and owned some fine pictures, bought abroad. Mrs Taylor was a dour Calvinistic lady whom her daughters detested. Mary had one sister, Martha, who was at Roe Head with her. Martha was a tremendously lively tomboy of a girl, nicknamed 'Little Miss Boisterous' by her schoolmates, always in trouble, always full of fun, whom everybody forgave and loved. (It was Mary, however, who was considered extremely pretty.) There were also four Taylor brothers, and the whole of the Taylor family argued and discussed all day and all evening, throwing out opinions on politics and religion and literature which would have made gentle Ellen's hair stand on end – and Mr Brontë's too, one

Haworth Main Street. 'The flag-stones with which the steep ascent is paved are placed end-ways, in order to give a better hold to the horses' feet.' (Mrs Gaskell, *Life*)

would imagine. Charlotte, however, enjoyed the Taylor hurly-burly. Charlotte almost revealed to Mary 'the world below', telling her about *The Young Men's Magazine*, which she produced with her brother Branwell, and promising to show her an example. This promise, however, she formally retracted, and could not be persuaded to tell any more. Whether she spoke in general more frankly to Mary than to Ellen we do not know, but guess that it was so, for Mary destroyed all Charlotte's letters to her, thinking it 'not safe' to keep them.

Of Charlotte at Roe Head we have accounts from both Ellen and Mary. Each has a real pathos of its own.

Mary was the first to see Charlotte when she arrived, dismounting from the covered cart, looking miserable and cold. Her dress was old, she was very small, she spoke with an Irish accent, she was so short-sighted she could not play games because she could not see the ball. At first the bigger girls thought her ignorant, because she knew no grammar and very little geography, but they soon found she knew things 'out of our range altogether'. Poetry she knew, and pictures, and could explain them well; she could 'make out', i.e. invent stories and characters, without any difficulty; her whole family was used to doing so, she said. 'I told her sometimes', said the practical Mary, 'they were like growing potatoes in a cellar.' She said sadly: 'Yes! I know we are!' She picked up every scrap of information concerning painting, sculpture, poetry, music, etc., said Mary, as if they were gold.

Ellen arrived at Roe Head a week after the beginning of term in 1831. The girls were just going out to play. She was not required to go with them, but ushered into the schoolroom and left alone, to settle down. Awestruck and homesick, she gazed about her at the books and the long table covered with a crimson cloth, and presently discerned something – yes, it was a girl – quietly weeping, crouched by the bay window. She advanced and uttered a word or two, confessing her own homesickness. Tears flowed from both, and from that moment the two girls were friends. Ellen is as severe as Mary about Charlotte's appearance; her exceeding thinness and want of complexion, her hair of soft silky brown screwed up in tight little curls so as to be 'dry and frizzy-looking', her 'dark, rusty, green stuff dress of old-fashioned make', all come under criticism. But of Charlotte as a person Ellen could not speak too highly. Her absolute rectitude, her earnest study, her story-telling powers, her great abilities which soon took her to the top of the school, her continual devotion to the duty of fitting herself to earn a livelihood, are all recorded as well as, again, her short sight and lack of physical strength.

At the close of her first half-year, Charlotte bore off three prizes. After three half-years, in July 1832, she left Roe Head, having gone through all the elementary teaching contained in its schoolbooks.

Before the month was out the faithful Ellen was writing to Charlotte asking for a description of how she had spent her time every day since leaving Roe Head. This was soon done, replied Charlotte, for an account of one day was an account of all. 'In the morning from nine o'clock till half-past twelve, I instruct my sisters and draw, then we walk till dinner, after dinner I sew till tea time, and after tea I either read, write, do a little fancy work or draw, as I please.'

This description of life at the Parsonage, which continued on the same lines for three years, gives a peaceful picture of Charlotte, now rising sixteen and equipped with a good formal education, living a quiet domestic life, passing on the benefits she had received to two young sisters. No doubt what it says is perfectly true, but its omissions are so great as to make the picture quite false. Scrupulous as always, Charlotte inserts the one word 'write'. This in fact covers an enormous amount of literary activity by Charlotte and her brother.

Obverse and reverse of silver medal won by Charlotte Brontë 'for the fulfilment of duties' at Roe Head, 1831–2

41

*Angria*　When Charlotte went to Roe Head, the children seriously debated the fate of their dream-world, and apparently decided to destroy it, for in the Christmas holidays of 1831, Charlotte wrote a tremendous poem describing the destruction of Great Glass Town by the Genii. The poem begins 'The trumpet hath sounded', continues in the metre of Byron's *Destruction of Sennacherib*, and seems to derive much from one of the fashionable pictures of John Martin, *Belshazzar's Feast*. Charlotte and Branwell soon retracted the destruction, but it was during Charlotte's absence that Emily and Anne broke finally away from Great Glass Town and withdrew to Gondal. Branwell, lonely without his collaborating sister, wrote two long treatises, one a series of letters in six volumes describing the visits of a young Englishman to Verdopolis, the other, entitled *The History of the Young Men* and furnished with a map, giving 'what myself, Charlotte, Emily and Anne really pretended did happen among the Young Men'. As soon as Charlotte returned permanently from Roe Head, she plunged into Angria with tremendous energy, and the years from 1832 to 1838 are crowded with Angrian productions. The saga now, thanks to Charlotte's increasing maturity, loses some of its childish flavour, resuscitations of dead characters and the like, and becomes a powerful romance; Rogue is discovered to be the black sheep of the noble Percy family, and develops into a Byronic hero, 'bright with beauty, dark with crime', who is eventually elevated into the Duke of Northangerland, Zamorna's hostile father-in-law. It is towards the end of this period that Charlotte introduces the character of Mina Laury as one of Zamorna's mistresses.

Aunt Branwell's teapot

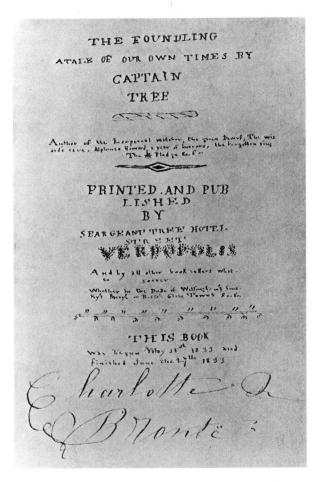

Title-page of 'The Foundling', one of Charlotte Brontë's youthful daydream stories (1833)

Early students of the Brontës, who knew little or nothing of these daydream writings, considered the lives of the Brontës cold and dreary. Later students, struck by the blazing fire of the invention, believed them to be happy. Neither statement is quite correct. From any cold or dreary scene Charlotte and Branwell could step instantly into a palace blazing with light, abounding with beauty dressed in velvet and diamonds engaged in an exciting story of love and war. But this feverish pleasure unfitted them for the ordinary relationships of the ordinary world, which by contrast struck them as stale, flat and unprofitable. Nothing in the real world ever came up to their expectations. Gondal had no radiant palaces, no diamonds, but it had passions of extreme intensity, which, however, Emily did not consider alien to the real world. The Gondal morals of Emily and Anne were the same as their Haworth morals; in Gondal no Zamorna flourished; evil deeds brought evil consequences in Gondal.

*Gondal*

43

In September 1832 Charlotte made her first visit to Rydings. Branwell escorted her there in the two-wheeled Haworth gig. He was in ecstasies about the house and grounds, thinking them a very Paradise, and Ellen observed how proud Charlotte was of her brilliantly expressive brother. In July the following year Ellen paid her first visit to Haworth. She won golden opinions there, even from Emily and Tabby, and these mutual visits were often repeated, continuing when Ellen moved to Brookroyd next year.

Haworth Parsonage: the entrance hall.
'There was not much carpet anywhere. . . . The hall floor and stairs were done with sand-stone, always beautifully clean, as everything was about the house; the walls were not papered, but stained in a pretty dove-coloured tint.'
(Ellen Nussey, *Charlotte's Early Life at Haworth*)

44

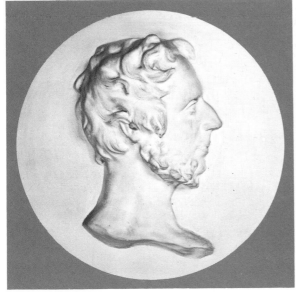

Medallion of Branwell Brontë by Joseph Bentley Leyland     Portrait of Mr Brontë, aged fifty-six

*Parsonage*

Ellen's later description of Haworth Parsonage, its inhabitants and manners, as she saw them in 1833, brings it all vividly before our eyes. The spotless cleanliness, the lack of carpet; the sandstoned hall floor and stairs, the walls not papered, but stained 'in a pretty dove-coloured tint'; hair-seated chairs and mahogany tables, bookshelves in Mr Brontë's study; the clock halfway up the stairs which Mr Brontë wound up every night on his way to bed, after conducting family prayers and locking the front door. The animals, the oatmeal porridge for breakfast, the pistol Mr Brontë fired out of the window each morning, the joyous rambles on the moors.

Mr Brontë appeared to Ellen venerable and courteous. At this time he already wore a high white cravat, which he covered himself by winding white sewing-silk over it; later – probably because he never removed one layer of silk before imposing another – this cravat reached remarkable dimensions. Aunt Branwell, thought Ellen, was a very small, antiquated old lady, whose huge caps, false front, pattens and gold snuffbox did not escape the visitor's shrewd eye.

*Personal appearances*

Best of all, Ellen closely describes the girls. The Brontë children were all small, like their mother. (The Haworth joiner who made their coffins affirms that Charlotte was 4 foot 9 inches, Emily the tallest at 5 foot 3 inches.) Emily at this time had acquired 'a lithesome graceful figure'. Like Charlotte, she lacked a good

45

complexion; her hair, a darker brown than Charlotte's, was in the same un-becoming tight curl and frizz as her sister's, but her eyes were beautiful – 'kind, kindling, liquid' eyes, which sometimes appeared dark blue, sometimes dark grey. Anne – 'dear, gentle Anne', as Ellen calls her – was quite different in appearance from her sisters. She had lovely violet-blue eyes, fine pencilled eyebrows and clear, almost transparent complexion; her hair was a pretty light brown, and fell on her neck in graceful curls.

Of Branwell, unfortunately, Ellen offers no description. Charlotte in the Angrian stories gives Patrick Benjamin Wiggins 'carroty' hair, but probably this

The parlour, Haworth Parsonage, today. The furniture is contemporary, but not all actually owned by the Brontës

(Above left) Emily Brontë, painted by Branwell

(Above right) Anne Brontë, watercolour by Charlotte

was a sisterly joke and his hair was dark red. I have myself seen, in County Down in 1932, a collateral descendant of Mr Brontë's family who had this dark red hair, and the large aquiline nose which appears in the medallion of Branwell sculptured later by his friend J.B. Leyland; the resemblance was indeed remarkable. When Ellen wrote this account of the Parsonage, after all its inhabitants were dead, Branwell had become a saddening subject, not to be dwelt upon. Ellen does, however, mention that he was at this time studying with his father and painting in oils, in preparation for what might, as all the family hoped, eventually be his profession of artist.

47

Sir Walter Scott

Although Charlotte never met an author until after she had become famous, – Emily and Anne never – she already knew them all in their works. A letter written in reply to Ellen's request for some recommendations for reading about this time cites ten excellent poets, including Pope 'though I don't admire him', six first-class biographies, four fine naturalists. 'Omit the Comedies of Shakespeare, the *Don Juan*, perhaps the *Cain* of Byron. . . . For fiction, read Scott alone; all novels after his are worthless.' Taste and book-knowledge are not out of reach, even in Haworth.

The 'gun' portrait of Branwell and his sisters (Anne and Charlotte at left, Emily at right), painted by Branwell

In 1835, Charlotte being nineteen, Branwell eighteen years old, the young Brontës began to try to put themselves in the way of earning their livelihood. As Charlotte explained to Ellen, 'Emily is going to school, Branwell is going to London, and I am going to be a Governess.' There followed, for three of them at least, seven years of honest and strenuous endeavour in the face of great unhappiness, ending for all in failure.

Mr Brontë's narrow income would scarcely suffice for Branwell to attend the Royal Academy Schools in London and Emily to attend Roe Head, so it was necessary for Charlotte to supplement it by her earnings. Miss Wooler offered her a post as teacher at Roe Head, the salary for which was to be partly paid by Emily's board and tuition. Charlotte preferred this to the prospect of private governessing, and she went to Roe Head with Emily in July 1835. Unfortunately, Emily could not endure the lack of liberty necessarily imposed by residence in a boarding school. She silently lost weight and colour, and in October left Roe Head. Anne took her place in January 1836. To Charlotte, Anne was always the little sister, and she was now a pupil; though there was a deep affection between them, there was not quite so close an intimacy as between Charlotte and her other sister.

Charlotte was desperately unhappy these first years at Roe Head. She did not really like children and was not one to suffer fools gladly; teaching a few ordinary

*Teaching*

49

girls in a quiet West Riding backwater, with no prospect of anything else before her, and no monetary gain after she had clothed Anne and herself, irked her proud aspiring spirit almost beyond endurance. It is clear from her replies to Ellen that Ellen's letters urged religious consolations upon her, and Charlotte struggled to bow her head and adopt these. But, 'I am *not like you*,' she cried in agony. 'If you knew my thoughts; the dreams that absorb me; and the fiery imaginations that at times eat me up and make me feel Society as it is, wretchedly insipid, you would pity and I daresay despise me.'

This language, this talk of 'evil wandering thoughts', must have seemed perplexing and exaggerated to the sedate Ellen, but it is now no mystery. When we observe that only a few days before the date of this letter Charlotte was writing an impassioned story about the Duke of Zamorna and Mina Laury, we can understand how she was torn between her sincere moral beliefs and her powerful urge to write of illicit amours. Her characterization in this story is really splendid; this girl of barely twenty from a remote country parsonage displays the difference between the pale Duchess of Zamorna in her quiet dress and Mina in black satin

Imaginary portrait from
Charlotte's sketchbook
(probably an Angrian character)

Robert Southey
in his youth, 1845

and ruby ear-rings, both women made equally unhappy by the man they love, with a skill greater and more subtle than that, say, of Ouida. Anyone who has daydreamed in spheres their normal beliefs forbid – and this is the essential nature of a Freudian daydream – and tried to break the habit, will know the keen agony of the effort, the glorious relief of its abandonment.

*Southey*

In this anguish Charlotte wrote to the poet Southey; the letter has not been preserved, but Southey sent a kindly reply, warning her (justly) of the dangers of daydream, and (infuriatingly) that literature cannot be the business of a woman's life and ought not to be; she had evidently sent him some specimens of her verse and prose. To this letter Charlotte replied most honourably and nobly, thanking the poet for his kind and wise advice and promising never to forget it. Nevertheless she continued, though perhaps less frequently, to write Angrian pieces, until at last, in 1839, she took the resolve to quit her 'world below', and wrote the tragic, noble, beautiful, untitled quarter-page which bids Angria's familiar landscapes, its well-loved faces and 'burning clime' a long farewell.

Diary note written by Emily on Branwell's birthday, 26 June 1837

In 1837, in consequence of her father's death and other domestic rearrangements, Miss Wooler moved her school to Dewsbury Moor; in the next months she was often absent on family business and relinquished her command to some extent to her sister Eliza; Charlotte's responsibilities increased. Charlotte detested the new location, and Anne's health at once began to fail there. Charlotte, who remembered all too well the illness and deaths of her elder sisters, was alarmed about Anne's condition, and thought Miss Wooler's attitude to it callous. She resented this lack of understanding so strongly that she had a sharp tiff with Miss Wooler. They made it up on Miss Wooler's initiative, who wept and declared her regard for Charlotte. Anne, however, left Dewsbury Moor in December 1837, having had two years' education under the Wooler régime.

Shibden Valley, the landscape visible from the back windows of Law Hill

Meanwhile, Emily this year took a post as governess in a girls' boarding-school of forty pupils, known as Law Hill, kept by a Miss Patchett at Southowram, on one of the many Pennine hills surrounding the town of Halifax. The account of her duties there is appalling. 'Hard labour from six in the morning until near eleven at night, with only one half-hour of exercise in between. This is slavery,' writes Charlotte: 'I fear she will never stand it.' How long Emily did actually stand it is in doubt; was it for six or for eighteen months? It is difficult to imagine her holding out for the longer period, yet her poem beginning: 'A little while, a little while, The noisy crowd are barred away', which seems clearly to relate to school life, is dated December 1838, so she may have done so. She continued to write poems, sometimes of Gondal, sometimes of Yorkshire, throughout this period. The most interesting feature of her stay is that Law Hill is not far from High Sunderland on the one hand, Shibden Hall on the other, two fine old houses each of which presently contribute to the setting of *Wuthering Heights*.

In the May of 1838 Charlotte left Dewsbury Moor. Her health and spirits had utterly failed her, and the doctor she consulted advised her that if she valued her life, she must return home. She did so, and was slowly restored to tranquillity.

Shibden Hall, near Halifax. The relative situation of Shibden Hall in the valley and High Sunderland on the moor corresponds to that of Thrushcross Grange and Wuthering Heights. Both houses are within walking distance of Law Hill

A cheering event at this time was probably the visit to Haworth of Mary and Martha Taylor. Mary played the piano, Martha chattered, Branwell laughed at her vivacity. It is possible, however, that it was at this time that Mary, to use a commonplace phrase, 'took a fancy' to Branwell, whereat he, perceiving this, despised her. This is referred to vaguely, no names mentioned, by Charlotte later, when warning Ellen not to show her feelings too strongly in similar circumstances.

*Nussey proposal*    Charlotte received three, almost four, proposals of marriage in her life; the first came in March 1839 from Ellen's brother, the Rev. Henry Nussey. This was a great temptation to Charlotte, as she confessed to Ellen, for Ellen could have made one of the household. But realizing that she could not feel towards Henry as she believed a woman ought to feel towards her husband, she refused him – very pleasantly, however, so that there were no hard feelings between them. Since Henry Nussey's diary reveals that he had made up his mind it was time he had a wife, and had already proposed to two other young ladies (whose fathers had rejected him), her decision was probably wise.

54

Wath Church, near Ripon, where Charlotte visited with the Sidgwick family when governess at Gateshead Hall, Stonegappe

Next month Anne, now nineteen, took a brave decision to venture forth and earn. She became governess in the family of Mrs Ingham, Blake Hall, Mirfield, and remained there for nine months.

Anne was indeed the most successful of the Brontë sisters in her governess attempts. She was milder, more ordinary, than the other two, and really liked children. If, however, we are to judge her teaching methods by those which Agnes Grey employed in Anne's novel of that name, we must find them psychologically deplorable. To barricade a child in a corner by a chair, or hold her down by strength of arm, insisting that she must repeat one word of her lesson before going out to the garden, to shake her, to pull her long hair and so on, are not excusable even by the total lack of support for the authority of the governess given her by the children's doting mother. No wonder the little wretches screamed.

In May Charlotte took a post as governess in Mrs Sidgwick's family, at Stonegappe near Skipton. In spite of the beauty of the surroundings she was bitterly unhappy there, bowed down under a weight of plain sewing, bored and unnerved by innumerable visitors, with no time to herself; as for the children, 'more riotous, perverse, unmanageable cubs never grew'. She made all the effort to please of which she was capable, but Mrs Sidgwick rebuked her so sharply that she cried. Characteristically, she much preferred Mr Sidgwick to his wife. She left the Sidgwicks in July.

The Brontës did not realize sufficiently at the time how terribly the curtailing of their liberty depressed them. If they had taught in day-schools, they could perhaps have endured the day, however unmanageable the cubs, by looking forward to the free evening. But to be always on show, never free, never able to choose, never alone, was more than their natures could endure; the ever-present sense of imprisonment fretted their nerves to breaking-point.

Charlotte received her second proposal of marriage a month after returning from Stonegappe. An Irish curate, the Rev. James Bryce, coming over with his vicar to spend the day with Mr Brontë, made Charlotte laugh by his Irish jokes, and a few days later sent her an ardent proposal by letter. Charlotte, amused but not unflattered, promptly refused him.

In September Charlotte and Ellen, after maddening delays from their respective families, managed to take themselves for a seaside holiday to Bridlington on the East Yorkshire coast. They were constrained by family friends to stay for a month at their cottage at Easton a few miles from the sea, but had a week, all they found they could afford, in Bridlington lodgings, alone. Charlotte discovered a deep passion for the sea, which she never forgot.

Skipton Castle. Stonegappe was a few miles distant

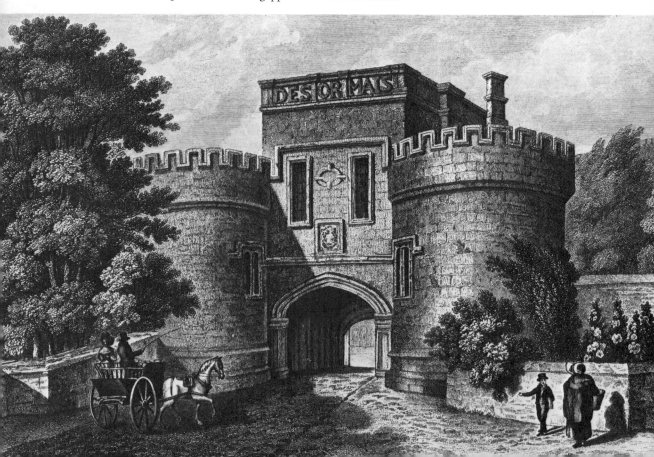

Bathing from the shore at Bridlington

Flossie, Anne's spaniel, drawn by Charlotte

Railway station at Keighley in the 1840s

*William*
*Weightman*
A brief spell of happiness was now enjoyed by the sisters while they were all at home together. This was due entirely to the presence of the Rev. William Weightman, who came to Haworth as Mr Brontë's curate in 1839.

The son of a Westmorland brewer, Weightman had a good classics degree from Durham University, and was a lively, handsome, agreeable young fellow, 'constitutionally cheerful', as Mr Brontë called him, a good preacher if a little above his Haworth hearers' heads, and conscientious about his parish work. The girls called him *Celia Amelia*; Charlotte painted his portrait and he sent them all Valentines, to which Charlotte replied in a rather lengthy set of verses. When he was to give a lecture in Keighley, he persuaded a married clerical colleague to entertain them all to tea and chaperon them for the evening; the whole party burst into Haworth Parsonage late that night after walking the four miles up the valley from Keighley, and Aunt was cross because the coffee she had prepared for the family was not enough to provide for the two additional clerics. This is really almost the only occasion when the Brontës enjoyed the normal social life of ordinary young people.

William Weightman flirted, agreeably and harmlessly, with every girl in sight, and there was the usual flutter and gossip in the neighbourhood which encircle a marriageable young bachelor, even sedate Ellen wanting to know what he thought of her. But Anne, dear gentle Anne, was deeply though silently affected. Emily, who gained the joking nickname of 'The Major' at this time by her close guardianship of her sisters, perhaps realized Anne's attachment, but apparently Charlotte did not. She described to Ellen how Weightman sat opposite to Anne in Church, sighing softly and looking out of the corners of his eyes to win her attention, but 'Anne is so quiet, her look so downcast, they are a picture.' The curate would be the better for a comfortable wife to settle him, she goes on, 'and you would settle him I believe – nobody else would'. But from Anne's own words we have the evidence of her feelings. Her quiet little poem *A Reminiscence* is deeply tragic.

> Yes, thou art gone! and never more
> Thy sunny smile shall gladden me . . .
> The lightest heart that I have known,
> The kindest I shall ever know.

But in August 1840 Anne went as governess to the family of the Rev. Mr Robinson, a country landowner at Thorp Green in the Plain of York; it was not Anne's destiny to be a happy wife.

Manuscript of a poem by
Emily, 1830

William Robinson, of Leeds, who
taught the Brontës painting

Branwell and Mr Weightman were good friends, and the curate's friendship
was for Branwell as for his sisters a short golden strand in life. For if his sisters
had been unhappy during the years 1835 to 1841, Branwell had been wretched.
This was the crucial period for Branwell, when everything went wrong for him,
and from being the bright star, the brilliant hope, of the Parsonage family, his
promise blurred and tarnished and he began to be viewed with apprehension.

Mr Brontë, perceiving his children's inclination towards art and their sterile
copying of engravings minutely, almost dot by dot, had for some time provided
them with lessons from an art master. In 1835, Branwell having apparently
decided upon art in preference to literature as a career, Mr Brontë paid for lessons
for him in painting from William Robinson of Leeds. In the early months of
*Branwell* the following year Branwell set off for London to join the Royal Academy
*in London* Schools. Aunt Branwell provided him with money, Robinson gave him intro-
ductions. A week or two later Branwell returned home, moneyless, without
having joined the Academy Schools or presented any of his letters of introduction.
His story was that he had been robbed at an inn before ever reaching London;
he had in fact visited an inn in Holborn kept by a noted pugilist, and enjoyed
the rackety life there.

60

The Castle Tavern,
Holborn, kept by the
pugilist Tom Spring

61

Why and how this astonishing disaster occurred was a question highly perplexing at first to Brontë biographers, but the answer to it probably emerges in an Angrian story, *Charles Wentworth's Visit to Verdopolis*, written by Branwell in May 1836, that is, shortly after his return from London. Wentworth's violent reaction to the sight of the capital city he had so long desired to see, quite overpowered him; 'his mind being overstrained the relapse was as strong as the spring'. He stretched himself upon a sofa, and listlessly dreamed away his time till dark. Next day he hesitated to enter the mighty buildings 'from instinctive fear of ending his pleasure by approaching reality'. This is the Nemesis of the daydreamer, and next day Wentworth is feeding his anxious, restless shrinking from reality on 'little squibs of rums'.

The account of Wentworth's reaction seems too near autobiography to be disregarded. Perhaps, too, Branwell saw the great paintings of the galleries and was daunted by the unlikelihood of his own talent reaching to such heights. The foolish lad was conceited, but saw that London was not Haworth.

Naturally after this rebuff from Fate (for a man's character is his Fate) Branwell turned back to his other love, literature. For the next four years he wrote copious Angrian histories in prose, and many Angrian and other pieces in verse, these culminating in his translation of all but one of the Odes of Horace, which he completed in 1840. This was a considerable achievement for a young man of twenty-three. Indeed, Branwell sometimes writes a line of such true lyric sweetness or employs an unusual metre so gracefully, that one can hardly credit his authorship of other poems of commonplace badness. Can the same man have written *The Epicurean's Song* –

> So seize we the present,
>     And gather its flowers,
> For, – mournful or pleasant –
>     'Tis all that is ours;
>         While daylight we're wasting,
>         The evening is hasting,
>     And night follows fast on vanishing hours.

– and the line: *A bleeding spirit oft delights in gore?*

A Haworth Temperance Society pledge signed by the Rev. Patrick Brontë and Branwell Brontë as witnesses

The Black Bull, Haworth, in the Brontës' day. The figure in the top hat on the left is said to be the Haworth stationer, John Greenwood ▶

During this period Branwell wrote to the editor of *Blackwood's Magazine*, and to William Wordsworth. From neither did he obtain a reply. This is not surprising when one reads his letters, for they are conceited, impertinent, bullying and wild almost to the point of madness.

It was during the years 1836 to 1838, while Branwell was at home, that he began to take part in Haworth activities. He played the church organ, taught in Sunday school, was made a Freemason and secretary to the local temperance society. He also became friendly with the parish sexton, John Brown, and this was perhaps less desirable. John Brown was an original character in his own right; bookish and intelligent, he had a bold speech and a robustly permissive philosophy of life perfectly proper for a man in his own sphere, but not such as the relatives of a rather weak son of the Parsonage in 1837 could easily approve. Branwell, we are told, had a voice of ringing sweetness, and his use of English was so perfect as to give delight; he was welcome everywhere for his conversation, and one of the places which welcomed him too often was the Black Bull.

Mrs Kirby, as painted by
Branwell

*Bradford studio*    Since literature proved unrewarding, Branwell turned to art again, and by May 1838 was installed in rooms and a studio in Bradford, found for him by the Rev. William Morgan. Here he painted portraits of his landlord, Mr Kirby, and his wife, and of various Bradford notabilities introduced by Mr Morgan. Opinions vary as to the merit of Branwell's painting. It has been said that his anatomy is vague and his knowledge of colour-harmony poor, but in some of his portraits, notably that of Mrs Kirby, he seems to catch a likeness. His time in Bradford was a happy one for Branwell. He enjoyed the society of the young men, like himself would-be writers and painters, who flourished about the town, especially that of Joseph Bentley Leyland, the Halifax sculptor, who had achieved the success in London which Branwell lacked. But Bradford proved too small a city to provide a living for all these aspirants, and in 1839 Branwell was at home in Haworth again, being rebuked by his family – if we may judge from an Angrian story – for liking his glass of an evening 'the same as another'.

*Tutor*    Presently, in 1840, perhaps stimulated to fresh effort by William Weightman, he went as tutor to the family of Mr Robert Postlethwaite, magistrate and fox-hunter, in Broughton-in-Furness. On his way there two unlucky experiences befell Branwell. The coach passed the Clergy Daughters' School at Cowan Bridge, which revived all his sorrow for his two lost elder sisters. Then in the

The industrial West Riding in the
mid-nineteenth century; Bradford
from the south-east

Joseph Bentley Leyland, of Halifax, a
sculptor and one of Branwell's
closest friends

(Left) John Brown, the Haworth sexton, by Branwell. 'Old Knave of Trumps' (Branwell, *Letter* from Broughton-in-Furness) (Right) Hartley Coleridge, son of the poet Samuel Taylor Coleridge. He advised Branwell 'to make literature his life'

Kendal Inn he fell in with a party of gentlemen who drank themselves and him under the table. He described this riotous party to John Brown in an excited (and notorious) letter beginning: 'Old Knave of Trumps'. While at Broughton Branwell wrote to Hartley Coleridge, the son of the poet, a polite and reasonable letter which led to an invitation to visit Hartley at Ambleside. There was much similarity between Hartley and Branwell, in smallness of stature, love of literature, daydream world – Hartley's was named Ejuxria – and general failure. Hartley advised Branwell to make literature his life, and Branwell never forgot this. Later, Branwell meeting by chance 'a poet friend' went off with him on a prolonged carousal and had to be fetched back to Broughton, ignominiously drunk. Inquiries from his pupils, the two young Postlethwaite boys, brought to light Branwell's habit of occupying their lesson time by sketching and telling them stories to match the drawings. He was dismissed, but contrived to make himself appear at home as the injured party, and the girls, with their bitter experiences as governesses, of course believed him.

Keeper, Emily's dog, drawn
by Emily

(Below left) Letter to Ellen
Nussey from Charlotte Brontë

(Below right) Hero, a hawk
kept as a pet, painted by Emily

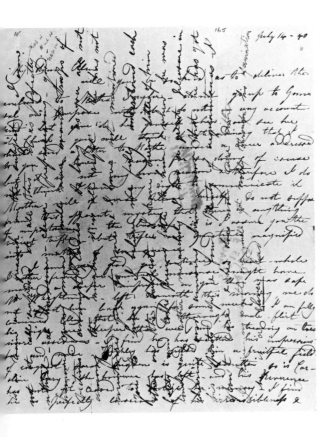

*Railway clerk*     A few months later (September 1840) Branwell obtained a situation as clerk at the station at Sowerby Bridge, in the Calder Valley, on the new Leeds–Manchester Railway. Next March, Branwell was transferred to the station at Luddenden Foot. Nowadays Sowerby Bridge is a much larger place than Luddenden Foot; whether it was so then is uncertain. To Ellen, innocently offering congratulations on Branwell's promotion, Charlotte replied: 'it *looks* like getting on at any rate'. Her italics made this sound a little dubious. Luddenden Foot is not far from Halifax, where the Leylands lived. In his better moments Branwell walked the beautiful Calder Valley and its surrounding hills with Joseph Bentley Leyland, his well-behaved brother Francis Alexander Leyland, who helped Branwell to get some of his poems printed in the *Halifax Guardian* and later became his biographer, and Francis Grundy, a railway engineer. All these were Branwell's sincere and lasting friends. Unfortunately, at Luddenden Foot he fell in with a

The Calder Valley, with Sowerby Bridge lying in the centre

Lord Nelson Inn, Luddenden, frequented by Branwell. 'I would rather give my hand than undergo again . . . the malignant yet cold debauchery . . . which too often marked my conduct there.' (Branwell, *Letter*)

set of young hardheaded millowners with whom he drank and quarrelled in the Lord Nelson Inn.

A year later, in March 1842, Branwell was dismissed by the railway company for an irregularity in his accounts, which were some eleven pounds short. He was not accused of dishonesty, but simply of constant carelessness. His frequent absences from the station, and his notebooks, which when examined by the railway officials revealed a compound of railway notations and Angrian and Yorkshire poems and drawings, confirmed the justice of this view.

Meanwhile, in March 1841, Charlotte, restored to health, bravely made another attempt at governessing, this time with the White family of Upperwood House, Rawdon, Leeds. Although much burdened with sewing, she was not altogether unhappy there. She liked Mr White and after a time came to like Mrs White (though she thought her of low extraction), and the children were not 'such little devils incarnate' as her previous pupils. Moreover, the parent Whites were often away, which was a relief, and there was a fat baby which Charlotte almost became fond of. She demanded and obtained three weeks' holiday in July, and it was during this holiday that with Emily – Anne was away at Thorp Green – Charlotte began to hatch the project of commencing a school of their own. Thinking that the East Riding of Yorkshire was perhaps less well provided with schools than the industrial West, they believed the neighbourhood of Bridlington might provide a suitable site, and Aunt offered a loan of £100 to finance the scheme. Through the next six months the possibility of this project swayed back and forth. Miss Wooler, whose school was now in some confusion, offered it to Charlotte and promised to lend her the necessary furniture. Charlotte wrote an acceptance, but the matter hung fire.

Then suddenly in September Charlotte wrote to her Aunt an extremely businesslike and persuasive letter, imparting a plan which the Whites and other friends had suggested and approved. It was that Charlotte and Emily should go abroad for a few months to acquire a thorough familiarity with French, improve in German and even get a dash of Italian, thus adding immensely to their qualifications for the instruction of pupils. Anne might take her turn at some future period. Martha Taylor was at a school at Kockleburg outside Brussels, too expensive for the Brontës, but the English Episcopal clergyman (whose brother was not unknown to Haworth) in that city would no doubt find them a school equally respectable though less showy. As Aunt liked to do things handsomely and was not fond of making shabby purchases, the scheme might well appeal to her – and so on.

Thus wrote Charlotte, but there was a deeper motive, confessed only to Ellen, which incited her. Mr Taylor having died that year, Mary Taylor had been journeying in Belgium and Holland with her brother Joe. Her letter to Charlotte spoke of exquisite pictures and venerable cathedrals.

> I hardly know what swelled to my throat as I read her letter . . . such a great thirst to see, to know, to learn. . . . I was tantalized with the consciousness of faculties unexercised. . . . A fire was kindled in my very heart which I could not quench. . . . I so longed to become something better than I am.

Aunt (astonishingly) agreed to the Brussels scheme. The Wooler suggestion was abandoned. After much correspondence it was settled that Charlotte and

Chartists' demonstration in London, 1842

Emily should become boarders at the Maison d'Education pour les Jeunes Demoiselles kept by Mme Heger-Parent at 32, Rue d'Isabelle, Brussels. Charlotte left Rawdon on Christmas Eve. In February 1842 Mr Brontë escorted Charlotte and Emily, first to London, where they stayed at the very masculine Chapter Coffee House in Paternoster Row for three days, were joined by Mary and Joe Taylor, and saw the sights. On Saturday morning the party took the steam-packet to Ostend, and finally, reaching Brussels on Monday night, the Brontës presented themselves at the Pensionnat Heger on Tuesday morning. Charlotte had begun the great adventure of her life.

A few years ago I asked Mme Beckers-Heger, the grand-daughter of the 1842 Hegers, whether the name was pronounced in French style, as though it had an acute accent on the first 'e', and if so, should such an accent be placed there in writing the name. She replied that Heger should be pronounced in French style, but written without an accent; such an accent was in fact 'une fantaisie'.

Constantin Heger and Zoë Parent were by no means schoolteachers of a humdrum type. Constantin's father, a rich jeweller, lent a large sum to a friend and lost it. He was ruined. Constantin's training to be a barrister was therefore broken off; he spent some time in Paris, returned to Belgium to take part in the Revolution of 1830, married, lost his wife and little daughter in a cholera epidemic, and began to teach in the boys' school, the Athénée Royal. Zoë Parent's father was a French *émigré*. His sister, known in the family as 'la tante de Charleville', was a nun in a convent in Charleville and escaped in romantic circumstances when a revolutionary army attacked the town. It was she who began the girls' school, which her niece continued. Zoë and Constantin met at the house of a mutual schoolmistress friend, and their similar belief in the high value of education brought them together. By 1842 they had been married six years and had three children; Mme Heger had made a considerable success of her school, which was now housed in the Rue d'Isabelle, while M. Heger was making a reputation for himself as an exceptionally fine teacher of literature in the Athénée Royal, which had now moved to premises overlooking the garden of his wife's school. Living at Number 32, as he did, he was able to give lessons there in the intervals of his work at the Athénée. Since 'dévouement absolue' to the pupils' interest was one of the requisites he defined as essential to the teacher's work, the high quality of his instruction can be imagined.

For reasons which will appear later, the portrait of M. Heger which until recently was all English readers were allowed to see of him showed him as a benign elderly man, aged somewhere in the sixties. But in 1842 when Charlotte knew him M. Heger was thirty-three and his wife thirty-seven. Mme Beckers-Heger most kindly gave me a print of a family picture of the Hegers in 1847, painted by Ange François, which shows Monsieur turning impetuously away to the side, while Madame sits serene and composed amid her children, of whom there were by that time six.

Charlotte draws vivid portraits of M. and Mme Heger, both in her letters and later in her novels. Monsieur, dark, choleric, irritable, a man of powerful mind and a stern, able teacher, but 'a little black ugly being', capable of looking at times like an insane tomcat or delirious hyena; capable also, however, of showing great kindness and taking endless trouble. Impartial observers say that Madame was discreet, reserved, cool, composed, dignified, benevolent, extremely capable and practical, just the kind of woman to exasperate the intense, romantic Charlotte. From the first, too, Charlotte disliked the surveillance which was then a normal feature of a continental school. Madame's felt slippers, her sudden unexpected appearances, aroused not only her resentment but her contempt.

But indeed the Hegers showed the Brontës much benevolence. Charlotte's letters of inquiry, describing herself and Emily as the daughters of a minister of

The Heger family, painted by Ange François in 1847, i.e. five years after Charlotte met them. ▶
M. Heger, wearing the famous spectacles, is on the left, his wife in the centre

religion desirous of improving themselves in order to teach others, awoke strong sympathy in the Hegers' hearts. Charlotte and Emily paid no extras, and Monsieur, noting their age – Charlotte twenty-six, Emily twenty-four – put them on a special course and gave them lessons himself. These lessons caused jealousy among the other pupils, for Monsieur was a great person in his wife's establishment. Several of the French *thèmes* (essays) which Charlotte and Emily wrote for him have been printed in the *Brontë Society Transactions*, with M. Heger's criticisms; these comments are illuminating, and show an exceptional understanding and feeling for language. Interestingly enough, Emily did not get on well with M. Heger, but he thought she had the better mind of the two sisters – a mind like a man's, said he; she might have been a great navigator.

*Pensionnat Heger* Charlotte was at first extremely happy at the Pensionnat Heger. To begin with, Brussels is a beautiful city by any standard; to a girl brought up on Industrial Revolution architecture it must have appeared a revelation. The Rue Royale, the Parc, the magnificent Grande Place, must have proved sources of deep enjoyment to her.

# MAISON D'ÉDUCATION
## Pour les jeunes Demoiselles,

**Sous la direction**

DE MADAME HEGER-PARENT,

Rue D'Isabelle, 32, à Bruxelles.

Cet établissement est situé dans l'endroit le plus salubre de la ville.

Le cours d'instruction, basé sur la Religion, comprend essentiellement la Langue Française, l'Histoire, l'Arithmétique, la Géographie, l'Écriture, ainsi que tous les ouvrages à l'aiguille que doit connaître une demoiselle bien élevée.

La santé des élèves est l'objet d'une surveillance active : les parents peuvent se reposer avec sécurité sur les mesures qui ont été prises à cet égard dans l'établissement.

Le prix de la pension est de 650 francs, celui de la demi-pension est de 350 francs, payables par quartiers et d'avance. Il n'y a d'autres frais accessoires, que les étrennes des domestiques.

Il n'est fait aucune déduction pour le temps que les élèves passent chez elles dans le courant de l'année. Le nombre des élèves étant limité, les parents qui désireraient reprendre leurs enfants, sont tenus d'en prévenir la directrice trois mois d'avance.

Les leçons de musique, de langues étrangères, etc., etc., sont au compte des parents.

Le costume des pensionnaires est uniforme.

La directrice s'engage à répondre à toutes les demandes qui pourraient lui être adressées par les parents, relativement aux autres détails de son institution.

**OBJETS À FOURNIR :**

Lit complet, bassin, aiguière et draps de lit.
Serviettes de table.
Une malle fermant à clef.
Un couvert d'argent.
Un gobelet.

Si les élèves ne sont pas de Bruxelles, on leur fournira un lit garni, moyennant 34 francs par an.

Prospectus of the Pensionnat Heger. 'This is a large school . . .' (Charlotte, *Letter*)

Hôtel de Ville, Brussels.
'Brussels is a beautiful city.'
(Charlotte, *Letter*)

Then, the Pensionnat Heger was extremely well conducted. At first there appear to have been some twelve boarders and forty *externes* (day boarders), but later Charlotte mentions 'almost ninety' pupils. The orderly bustle of the large classes, the seven visiting masters, the strange rules, the end-of-term examinations, the interesting language, the air of confidence about the place, above all the contact with the really fine mind of M. Heger, seemed to bring sunshine into her life. On the other hand, by despising the three French mistresses, despising the solid Belgian girls, despising Catholicism, despising Madame's surveillance, Charlotte maintained a feeling of cheerful superiority.

What Emily felt, she kept to herself. She worked like a horse, she improved her music, but when invited out to the homes of English residents or to Kockleburg, she sat silent in a corner and was universally unpopular – except with one or two very young pupils, who preferred her to Charlotte.

Presently the Hegers proposed that the Brontës should not return home in September, but remain at the Pensionnat for another half-year, Emily to teach music, Charlotte to teach English. For these services they were to receive board and tuition free of charge, but no salaries. Charlotte was inclined to accept.

75

But the Brontës' lives were not destined to sunshine. At home in Haworth, William Weightman died of cholera – and when one reads of the sanitation arrangements in Haworth at that time, one is not surprised – in early September. A month later, Martha Taylor – merry, tomboyish Martha – died at Kockleburg of the same disease. Before the Brontës were well recovered from this shock, Aunt Branwell fell ill with an internal obstruction, and died on 29 October. The Brontës in Brussels did not hear of this loss until early November, too late to attend Aunt's funeral. They left for home by the packet on the following Sunday, for Branwell was alone at home with Papa, and the two men could not be left to cope by themselves.

With them the Brontës took a letter from M. Heger to Mr Brontë, recommending that the girls should return to Brussels for another year to complete their studies, when a position at the Pensionnat could probably be offered, at least to one of them. A letter in affectionate terms from Mme Heger to Charlotte followed. It could not be doubted that both the Hegers wished sincerely for the Brontës' return.

Accordingly in January 1843 Charlotte took the decision she afterwards so bitterly regretted. Anne would return to Thorp Green, and Branwell too had secured a post there, as tutor to Mr Robinson's young son. Emily would remain at the Parsonage to look after Papa. Charlotte was free to return to Brussels. She was to undertake some tuition, it was now arranged, and for this receive free board and a small salary.

(Left) The Pensionnat Heger from the Rue d'Isabelle

M. Heger in middle life

She went eagerly and joyously. But everything at the Pensionnat now turned to misery for her. A teacher is not a pupil. Teaching rebellious Belgian girls, keeping class discipline, was, one may surmise, hard and distasteful work for any little foreigner whose looks and attire were insignificant, and particularly so for the sensitive Charlotte. There were now no more lessons from M. Heger, though she gave English lessons to himself and his brother-in-law. The Hegers invited her to use their private sitting-room as her own, but she could not bring herself to intrude upon their privacy. The three French mistresses she still found detestable. Moreover, Mme Heger seemed now to turn against her, so that Charlotte, disillusioned, likened her to an apparently rosy sugar-plum in reality made of coloured chalk. After a time: 'I fancy I begin to perceive the reason of this mighty distance and reserve,' wrote Charlotte to Ellen: 'It sometimes makes me laugh and at other times nearly cry.'

The truth was that Charlotte, at first quite unconsciously, not in the least realizing the nature of her feeling, had fallen in love with M. Heger. To her he was a Zamorna, dominant, imperious, a man whose will was law, but a Zamorna Brusselized, respectablized, above all *real*: a real man with chalk on his fingers, who smoked cigars. Mme Heger, worldly wise and fully aware of her husband's

77

attractions – his girl pupils were all too apt to adore him – perceived Charlotte's infatuation and deplored it. The future of her school, and thus of herself, her husband, her children, depended on the complete absence of all scandal, and she was no doubt much exasperated by this young foreigner's silliness. When Charlotte offered her resignation, she would gladly have accepted, but her husband vehemently forbade Charlotte to leave. Eventually, however, Charlotte took her decision, and arranged to leave Brussels on New Year's Day, 1844. Mme Heger escorted her to the boat at Ostend.

*Charlotte's letters*

The nature of Charlotte's feeling for M. Heger was at one time much disputed, but in view of the letters she wrote to him in the next two years it can no longer be in doubt. The first of the series is lost, but she refers to it in July 1844. I translate:

> I know that it is not my turn to write to you. . . . Ah, Monsieur! I once wrote you a letter that was less than reasonable, because sorrow was at my heart; but I shall do so no more. . . . I refrain from uttering a single complaint for your long silence – I would rather remain six months without receiving news from you than add one grain to the weight which overwhelms you. . . . It hurts to say goodbye, even in a letter.

This, though fervid, is reasonable, and refers to a pact obviously made with M. Heger as to the frequency of mutual letters, but as the months go by and Charlotte's unhappiness increases, and letters from M. Heger – who was a man of honour and moreover in love with his wife – did not come, her intensity grows. In October she asks whether he has heard from her in May and August.

The Pensionnat Heger and its garden, from the rear

Mme Heger in 1886. 'Always cool, and always reasoning.' (Charlotte, *Letter*)

(Right) M. Heger in 1886; but this was forty-four years after Charlotte met him

> For six months I have been awaiting a reply from Monsieur – six months' waiting is very long, you know. However, I do not complain, and I shall be richly rewarded for a little sorrow if you will now write a letter. . . .

Even by the following January no letter had come, and Charlotte speaks of 'the torments which I have suffered for eight months'.

> Day and night I find neither rest nor peace. . . . If my master withdraws his friendship from me entirely, I shall be altogether without hope.

By November 1845 she cries out in despair:

> To forbid me to write to you, to refuse to answer me, would be to tear from me my only joy on earth. . . . When day by day I await a letter, and when day by day disappointment comes . . . I lose appetite and sleep – I pine away.

No wonder that Mrs Gaskell, Unitarian minister's wife in the reign of Queen Victoria, when shown these epistles, blenched, and later exclaimed in horror: 'Those letters!' She gave only two carefully selected, very decorous extracts from them, and one must presume that it was because of this uncomfortable discovery and what was regarded then as the need to conceal it for the sake of Charlotte's reputation, that portraits of M. Heger at an elderly age were the only ones promulgated this side of the Channel.

79

On the edge of the last letter M. Heger carelessly noted the name and address of a shoemaker, in pencil. The four letters were torn across, then stitched together again. It is a tradition in the Heger family that Constantin eventually tore them and threw them in the wastepaper-basket, and that Zoë then withdrew and repaired and kept them. Perhaps she thought them interesting, perhaps she thought they might be useful. At any rate, the Hegers behaved honourably about these then-so-embarrassing documents. They were not made available for public study until 1913 (seven years after the death of Charlotte's husband), when the Hegers' son, Dr Paul Heger, presented the letters freely to the British Museum.

Meanwhile, M. Heger – one cannot but think, severely but wisely – did not write to Charlotte, and she herself wrote him no more. Through all that happened at Haworth in the years after the Brussels adventure, this secret anguish of Charlotte's gnawed at her heart and darkened her view of life.

*Mr Brontë's sight*

When she returned home in January 1844, she felt her enthusiasm tamed, her eager hopes of life broken; and Haworth seemed a lonely, quiet spot, buried away from all the world. She decided sensibly that her need was for action, and revived the project of a Brontë school. But Mr Brontë, she discovered, was now losing his sight by cataract and it was impossible to leave him. It may be unjust to Mr Brontë to wonder if there were another reason, but in the previous October a letter of his to a Haworth businessman who with his wife had called upon him,

Part of a letter from Charlotte to M. Heger, 8 January 1845. 'Jour et nuit je ne trouve ni repos ni paix, . . .' Mme Heger's stitches can be clearly seen

Haworth Parsonage as it is now, in the evening, from the graveyard. The west (right) wing was added in 1881

mentions 'false reports' referring to 'a lotion for my eyes', the smell of which 'slanderers' have ascribed 'to a smell of a more exceptionable character'. Whether in fact Mr Brontë, with Aunt Branwell dead, Charlotte, Branwell and Anne away and only the reserved (perhaps indifferent) Emily at home, had been taking a drop of whisky, or not, will never be known. The cataract was undoubted, and Charlotte felt she could not leave him.

After a few months at home, however, and a cheering visit to Ellen, Charlotte began to believe that a school for a limited number of young ladies might be run in the Parsonage itself, with building additions if the scheme proved successful. Aunt's Will had left each girl a little capital, which could perhaps be thus wisely invested. Circulars were printed; Ellen handed them round, Charlotte wrote to previous employers and possible parents. No pupils, however, emerged. The bleak situation of Haworth was probably the deterrent, and not Branwell, though his behaviour later clinched the abandonment of the scheme.

Mary Taylor, whose active enterprise Charlotte envied, went off to New Zealand with her youngest brother. Henry Nussey, appointed Vicar of Hathersage, married a bride with money. While he was on his honeymoon Ellen stayed at

### The Misses Bronte's Establishment

FOR

### THE BOARD AND EDUCATION

OF A LIMITED NUMBER OF

### YOUNG LADIES,

## THE PARSONAGE, HAWORTH,

NEAR BRADFORD.

#### Terms.

|  | £. | s. | d. |
|---|---|---|---|
| BOARD AND EDUCATION, including Writing, Arithmetic, History, Grammar, Geography, and Needle Work, per Annum, .. .. .. .. .. .. .. | 35 | 0 | 0 |
| French, German, Latin     .. .. each per Quarter, .. .. .. | 1 | 1 | 0 |
| Music, Drawing,     .. .. each per Quarter, .. .. .. | 1 | 1 | 0 |
| Use of Piano Forte, per Quarter, .. .. .. .. .. .. | 0 | 5 | 0 |
| Washing, per Quarter, .. .. .. .. .. .. | 0 | 15 | 0 |

Each Young Lady to be provided with One Pair of Sheets, Pillow Cases, Four Towels, a Dessert and Tea-spoon.

A Quarter's Notice, or a Quarter's Board, is required previous to the Removal of a Pupil.

Prospectus of the proposed Brontë School

Birthday note, dated 30 July 1845, by Emily Brontë. It was the custom of Emily and Anne to write on Emily's birthday diary notes describing their activities, to be opened four years later. 'By mistake we have opened the paper on the 31st instead of the 30th.'

his vicarage to prepare it for the happy couple. Charlotte, invited to Hathersage, hesitated, but when Anne, in Haworth for a short holiday, decided not to return to the Robinsons', Charlotte was set free; she travelled to Hathersage and stayed there with Ellen for a fortnight.

Hathersage in Derbyshire is not a large village, but this visit had two interesting results in Charlotte's life. She used its Peak scenery as the landscape for the Rivers' cottage in *Jane Eyre*, and as, in the church on the hillside, there is a grave celebrating the Eyre family, landowners in the district, it seems highly probable that Jane's name came from there.

*Eyre tomb*

Reaching Haworth from Hathersage at ten o'clock on a Saturday night, Charlotte found Branwell unexpectedly at home, ill. This was probably a euphemism for *drunk*, for Charlotte wrote later, to Ellen: 'He is so, very often, owing to his own fault.' It seems that Branwell in this state was too familiar to produce any great shock, but when Charlotte heard its present cause she was shocked indeed. The Robinson family having gone on holiday to Scarborough, Branwell had come home, and had received there a note from Mr Robinson, sternly dismissing him, on the grounds that his proceedings at Thorp Green had

*Branwell dismissed*

been bad beyond expression, and charging Branwell on pain of exposure to break off instantly and for ever all communication with every member of the family.

This tenebrous affair has caused endless speculation. Branwell declared he loved Mrs Robinson passionately and she him; Mr Robinson, he said, was an unkind husband, detested Branwell, and had made a clause in his Will depriving his wife of all his wealth if she married Branwell. So Branwell *said*. The last statement was proved totally false by Mr Robinson's Will when he died the following year, for it contained no such clause. Nor did Mrs Robinson show any sign of wanting to marry Branwell; she may have sent him money, but she married a certain Sir Edward Scott the moment his wife died. One is tempted, knowing Branwell's capacity for lying, to regard the whole story as invention. But Mrs Robinson may perhaps have been a silly woman who liked to hear Branwell talk, and encouraged him without realizing how serious the affair was to him. While the family were in Scarborough, Mr Robinson bought his wife an expensive shawl and brooch, so evidently he attached no blame to her. Did Anne decide to leave the Robinsons because she saw her brother's entanglement, or because she declined to be responsible for the intrigue which one Robinson daughter was carrying on with an actor, with whom she shortly afterwards eloped? (The Robinson girls wrote to Anne and even visited her, after she left them.) Mr Robinson's letter was posted in Scarborough the day after the arrival there of his young son, who had remained in Thorp Green with Branwell. Had Branwell in fact committed some wrongful act with or towards this son, who was drowned unmarried in his thirties? Was the Mrs Robinson affair a cover-story – invented by Branwell to conceal something even more sordid – which he afterwards came to believe himself?

Whatever the truth of the matter, it accomplished the ruin of Branwell. From the time of his dismissal onwards, he drank, got into debt, took opium, wrote wild letters, illustrated by wild sketches, to his Halifax friends, occasionally begged Grundy to find him employment but made no real attempt to secure any, dozed about the Parsonage in a drunken stupor by day, raged and ranted by night, and in general behaved with such feverish irresponsibility as to bring continual disquiet and distress to the Parsonage.

What Anne thought of this is revealed in her pathetic little poem, *Domestic Peace*, where she laments its absence from 'the house so drear'.

Charlotte turned angrily against her brother. In a very chilly letter sent to Branwell from Brussels she had already shown that she distrusted him. Now she tells Ellen that he is an impediment to all happiness, his bad habits are deeply rooted, while he is at home she will invite no one to come and share its discomfort, only the absolute want of means checks him (from drink, understood), no good can be said of him, she fears indeed 'he will never be fit for much'. This harsh judgment of a once adored brother must have been exacerbated by the wretched similarity between her own affairs and Branwell's. Both, it seemed, loved where society said they should not. Charlotte ate her heart out in stern silence; Branwell screamed his love in drunken spoutings, all over Haworth.

Emily's reaction is not so clear. In one of the diary notes which she and Anne wrote to each other on their birthdays, Emily states cheerfully that she is quite contented for herself, and that they are all in decent health, 'with the exception of B., who, I hope, will be better and do better, hereafter'. This calm comment, however, is dated only a few days after Branwell's dismissal, when serious disintegration had not yet set in. There is a tradition that Emily showed more kindness to Branwell than her sisters, that she was indeed Branwell's favourite sister. I see no evidence for this. In early Angrian stories Branwell speaks contemptuously of Emily and Anne. They never shared Angria with him, leaving Great Glass Town before this offshoot was developed. Boasting and lying, admittedly Branwell's sins, are peculiarly repugnant to a noble nature. It is true that Emily's poem, *Stanzas to –*, beginning *Well, some may hate and some may scorn*, was written in 1839, i.e. five years before the Robinson débâcle, and that it is about a Gondal character, but by 1839 Branwell had already failed in London and was failing in Bradford, and his habits were well established; while to transfer real emotion to a fictitious character in order to be able to express it to the full is a known mode of the creative writer.

> *Vain as thou wert, and weak as vain,*
> *The slave of falsehood, pride and pain,*
> *My heart has nought akin to thine –*
> *Thy soul is powerless over mine.*

Facsimile of manuscript of Gondal poem, 'There shines the moon', by Emily Brontë

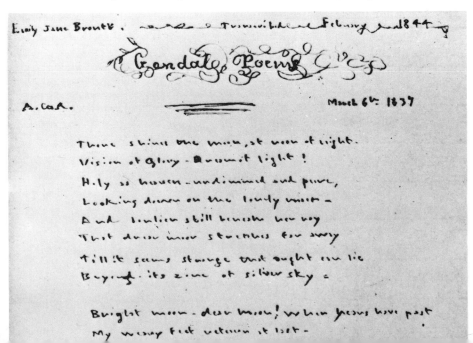

Rev. Arthur Bell Nicholls. 'I cannot for my life see those interesting germs of goodness in him you discovered; his narrowness of mind always strikes me chiefly.' (Charlotte, *Letter*, 1847)

It is Branwell and Emily's feeling for him, exactly. At the end of the poem, when the Gondalian is presumed dead, Emily shows pity and compassion, as indeed all must feel towards poor Branwell. But pity and compassion are not love.

Thus it came about that in 1845 the young Brontës were all at home together, living in domestic misery, all to some degree failures.

*Poems by*
*C., E. and A. Bell*

Then an event occurred, apparently very minor, which changed the course of their lives and added riches to English literature. Emily had been copying her poems into two notebooks, one for Gondal, one for non-Gondal, productions. Charlotte accidentally lighted upon one notebook and read its contents. Honour must always be paid to Charlotte for her instant conviction that these poems were quite out of the ordinary, terse, vigorous, genuine, with a peculiar music, 'wild, melancholy and elevating'. (These epithets are admirably just.) Emily was furious at this intrusion on her privacy; it took hours to soothe her, days to convince her that such poems merited publication. Meanwhile, Anne quietly produced some of her productions, which Charlotte estimated, again justly, as sweetly sincere. Charlotte added some of her own and the Brontës decided to bring out a volume of poems by all three sisters. Partly because they did not wish to incur the prejudice of contemporary critics against women writers, and partly to conceal the enterprise from Papa, Branwell and the West Riding in general, they veiled their own names under those of Currer, Ellis and Acton Bell. These pseudonyms, chosen scrupulously as being not positively masculine, have some interest. Mr Brontë had that year obtained a new curate, the Rev. Arthur Bell Nicholls. The connection of name may have been conscious or unconscious.

After a good deal of anxious correspondence on Charlotte's part about print, *Poems* paper, format and review copies, *Poems by Currer, Ellis and Acton Bell* appeared from Messrs Aylott and Jones in May 1846, paid for by ten guineas from each sister, later increased by one sum of five pounds. 'All of it that merits to be known', wrote Charlotte later, 'are the poems of Ellis Bell.' This is true, but the merit referred to is very great.

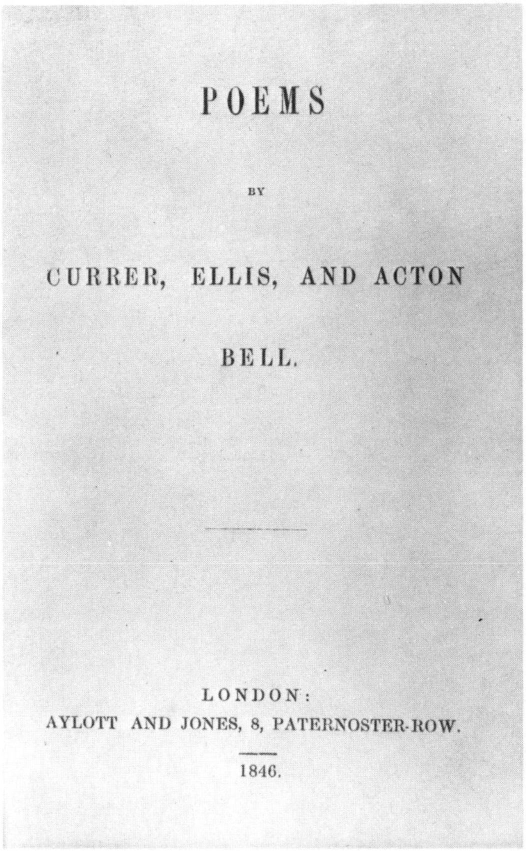

POEMS

BY

CURRER, ELLIS, AND ACTON

BELL.

LONDON:
AYLOTT AND JONES, 8, PATERNOSTER-ROW.

1846.

Title-page of *Poems* by Currer, Ellis and Acton Bell, 1846

High Withens, Haworth Moor. Ellen Nussey believed this was the original of Wuthering Heights. Its high, stormy situation corresponds exactly with that of the Heights

Emily Brontë was a 'space-sweeping soul', to use her own phrase about a philosopher; her thought on life, death, immortality, imagination, liberty, deity, had a depth and a breadth of vision comparable to that of Wordsworth or Shakespeare.

It has been the fashion to speak of her as a metaphysical poet, but I prefer to call her a pantheist; she saw the universe as a whole, and her vision comprehended the lark, the woolly sheep, the snowy glen, the nature of being and God Himself as all part of one great harmony. Nor can her thought be called speculative;

she writes with a majestic, almost casual, certainty. These tremendous themes, these minute observations, are both conveyed with an absolute simplicity of language; no purple patches of metaphor or simile, no elaboration of construction, no experiments with metre – one feels Emily would have thought any such artifices contemptibly vulgar. She merely says what she means in the clearest, hardest-hitting terms she can find. But if her metres are conventional and her words austere, her rhythms have a poetry so intense as to be deeply thrilling, in the most literal sense of that expression.

89

High Sunderland, Halifax, a seventeenth-century mansion not far from Law Hill, from which Emily borrowed some features for *Wuthering Heights*

*Death! that struck when I was most confiding . . .*
*Cold in the earth – and the deep snow piled above thee . . .*
*He comes with western winds, with evening's wandering airs,*
*With that clear dusk of heaven that brings the thickest stars . . .*

The critic of the *Athenaeum*, to his eternal honour, spoke of Ellis Bell's 'evident power of wing', but in spite of this and the expense of two pounds on advertising, the volume was a complete financial failure, only two copies being sold.

But to see one's words in print is a great stimulus to any writer. The three sisters now each began, or perhaps continued – at any rate finished – a novel.

*Agnes Grey*  Anne's novel was *Agnes Grey*, in which without ever raising her voice Anne quietly portrayed the horrors of a governess's life in all their awful detail. George Moore thought this story resembled a well-cut white muslin dress. Its mild, genteel tone, its pure language and absence of vivid colouring, even in the decorous love-affair with the curate, support his view, and its consistent realism about fond parents and foolish children certainly gives it a discriminating air.

Ponden Hall. This may have lent some features to Thrushcross Grange, but Shibden Hall
(see pp. 53, 54) seems more akin to that handsome establishment

Emily's solitary but superb masterpiece, *Wuthering Heights*, was so wild, so
fierce, that it positively frightened Charlotte. (The ferocity of the feelings described
does not, however, alarm the reserved Yorkshire people, who secretly believe –
not without cause – that they could be just as wild if they cared to let themselves
go.) The Earnshaws, farmers for three hundred years, live at the Heights on the
edge of the moors; the genteel, rather feeble landowners, the Lintons, live more
cosily at Thrushcross Grange down the valley. Mr Earnshaw brings home from
Liverpool a dark gipsy brat whom they call Heathcliff. Jealousy, hatred, a passion
almost too furious to be called love, ensue; the persecuted Heathcliff vanishes,
returns rich, finds his Cathy married to a Linton, determines to ruin both
families, and is only thwarted in the next generation by an honest decent love.
No finer depiction of landscape occurs in English literature than in *Wuthering
Heights*, save perhaps in the writings of Thomas Hardy; the moorland comes
before us in all moods, all weathers, painted in short, vivid, extremely beautiful
passages in each chapter.

*Wuthering
Heights*

# Jane Eyre
## by Currer Bell
### Vol. 1st

## Chap. 1st

There was no possibility of taking a walk that day.
We had been wandering indeed in the leafless shrubbery
an hour in the morning, but since dinner ( Mrs Reed
when there was no company, dined early) the cold win
wind had brought with it clouds so sombre, a rain so
trating that further out-door exercise was now out of
question.

I was glad of it; I never liked long walks — especia
on chilly afternoons; dreadful to me was the coming hom
in the raw twilight with nipped fingers and toes and a
saddened by the chidings of Bessie, the nurse, and humble
by the consciousness of my physical inferiority to Eliza, Joh
and Georgiana Reed.

The said Eliza, John and Georgiana were now cluster
round their Mamma in the drawing-room; she lay rec

Charlotte's novel, entitled *The Professor*, is, so to speak, a mirror-image of her
Brussels experiences. An English teacher in a Brussels school notices, admires,
at last loves, the shy little Anglo-Swiss pupil teacher. In the preface which
Charlotte later wrote for this, her first novel of real life, she tells how she had got
over any taste for 'ornamented and redundant' composition, and had come to
prefer what was plain and homely. She had decided that her hero should work
his way through life as she had seen real living men work theirs, that no sudden
turn should lift him to wealth and high station; 'as Adam's son he should share
Adam's doom, and drain but a mixed and moderate cup of enjoyment'.

These three novels were perseveringly obtruded upon various publishers without
success for a year and half. Then *Wuthering Heights* and *Agnes Grey* were accepted
by a minor publisher, T. C. Newby, for publication together in one volume on
condition that the authors advanced £50. But *The Professor*'s draught of saturnine
realism proved too bitter both for Newby and for other English publishers, and
the book was rejected by six firms. On the very morning when Charlotte took
Mr Brontë to Manchester to undergo his cataract operation, the rejected manuscript
returned to her yet once again.

But while Mr Brontë, the operation safely accomplished, lay upstairs in a
darkened room with a nurse in attendance, downstairs, alone, Charlotte began
to write *Jane Eyre*. One last despairing submission of *The Professor* to Messrs
Smith, Elder & Co. brought her a reply so courteous, so discriminating, so
encouraging, that when *Jane Eyre* was finished, Charlotte sent it to that firm.
Their reader, W. S. Williams, praised it to George Smith, who read it throughout
one Sunday, scarcely pausing to eat. The novel was accepted at once and was
published in October 1847, and immediately achieved a resounding popularity
which it has maintained ever since. Favourable reviews poured in; Thackeray
spent a whole day from his busy life reading it; G. H. Lewes praised it. (Later, even
Queen Victoria read 'that intensely interesting novel' to 'dear Albert'.)

The young girl struggling to maintain herself and her integrity against the world
is a theme frequent in romance. But Charlotte's version had a reality, a passion,
a nobility which sprang from her use of her own all too intensely real experiences
at Cowan Bridge and as a governess, and her superb presentation of her heroine.
Jane is a soul of fire, poor, plain, proud; a free human being with an independent
will who refuses to be overawed by the dominant, sophisticated, rich and powerful
Rochester, a real Zamorna – the accepted type of the spinster's hero, who needs
a powerful command to overcome her reluctance. The right of such a girl as
Jane to love, however poor, however plain, has attracted the warm sympathy of
girls always, though it shocked some Victorians and called down upon Charlotte
the accusation from Miss Rigby in the *Quarterly* that if the author of *Jane Eyre*
were a woman, she must be one who 'had forfeited the society of her sex'. But

◄ Opening page of the manuscript of *Jane Eyre*. Charlotte's novels
were always written in normal-size handwriting

(above left) Norton Conyers, probable original
Rochester's mansion, Thornfield, in *Jane Eyre*

(above right) Entrance to the 'madwoman's'
m

ght) Staircase of Norton Conyers

eft) Wycoller Hall, probably the original of
ndean, in *Jane Eyre*, where Rochester lived
r the fire at Thornfield

JANE EYRE.

An Autobiography.

EDITED BY

CURRER BELL

IN THREE VOLUMES.
VOL. I.

LONDON:
SMITH, ELDER, AND CO., CORNHILL.
1847.

Title-pages of first editions of
*Jane Eyre, Wuthering Heights* and
*The Tenant of Wildfell Hall*

this was only one dissentient voice; *Jane Eyre*'s triumph was practically complete.

Charlotte now ventured to tell her father of her literary attempt and to leave him a copy of her novel to read. After an amusing interview and a short perusal Mr Brontë burst in upon his daughters greatly excited, crying that Charlotte had written a novel, and that it was 'much better than likely'. Branwell, however, whose decline had now reached the level of begging the sexton for fivepence worth of gin, was never told of his sister's achievement.

By early December a second edition of *Jane Eyre* was called for. Charlotte, knowing nothing of the insane wife who made Thackeray's circumstances in this respect resemble Rochester's, dedicated this edition to the author of *Vanity Fair*, then publishing in monthly numbers. This released a further flight of rumours. In December *Wuthering Heights* and *Agnes Grey* appeared. Not well produced, with many printers' errors, the one was regarded as the product of a dogged, brutal and morose mind, the other as insipid, and both were received with indifference. But it was natural enough that curiosity should be roused by

WUTHERING HEIGHTS

A NOVEL,

BY

ELLIS BELL,

IN THREE VOLUMES.

VOL. I.

LONDON:
THOMAS CAUTLEY NEWBY, PUBLISHER,
72, MORTIMER St., CAVENDISH Sq.

1847.

THE TENANT

OF

WILDFELL HALL.

BY

ACTON BELL.

IN THREE VOLUMES.

VOL. I.

LONDON:
T. C. NEWBY, PUBLISHER,
72, MORTIMER STREET, CAVENDISH SQUARE.
1848.

these three mysterious Bells, their undetermined sex, their relationships, their problematical separate existence. In May a third edition of *Jane Eyre* was called for. Charlotte received £500 in all for this book.

Meanwhile, the sisters began to write their next novels. Of Ellis and Acton Bell, Charlotte wrote in her *Biographical Notice*: 'they were both prepared to try again'. If Emily indeed attempted another novel, only this hint of it remains. Charlotte was discouraged by Smith, Elder from remodelling *The Professor*, considered the Chartists as a theme but after some hesitation began *Shirley*. Anne worked hard to complete *The Tenant of Wildfell Hall*, and against Charlotte's wishes sent it to Newby. Charlotte indeed thought *The Tenant* a mistake; the rich drunkard Arthur Huntingdon is not Branwell, but his drunkenness is Branwell's, and the remarkably conscientious rendering of this decay which Anne thought her duty distressed her gentle spirit. Newby brought out the book in June 1848, and, thoroughly unscrupulous, advertised it in such a way as to imply that it was by the author (in the singular) of *Wuthering Heights* and *Jane Eyre*. Worse, he offered

*The Tenant* in these terms to an American firm, with whom Smith, Elder had already made an agreement for Currer Bell's next novel. Striving to remain calm, Smith, Elder naturally wrote with some heat to Haworth. Horrified by this suggestion of underhand dealing on their part, Currer and Acton decided to go *Visit to London* to London at once to confirm their separate identities. Emily refused to accompany them. On 7 July Charlotte and Anne packed a small box and sent it down to Keighley, after tea walked down there through a storm – Charlotte says of snow, Mrs Gaskell of thunder – and were whirled away to London by the night express. They put up at the Coffee House and presented themselves to George Smith at 65 Cornhill next morning.

After the first stunned surprise the firm of Smith, Elder responded gallantly. The Brontës were dined at Smith's house and presented to his mother and sisters, taken to the opera and to hear a celebrated preacher, spent Sunday evening with W. S. Williams's family, visited the Royal Academy and the National Gallery on Monday, and returned home on Tuesday utterly exhausted, but now firm friends with their publishers. Smith, Elder bought up the remainder of the *Poems*

(Above left) W.S. Williams, second-in-command at Smith, Elder's. 'A pale, mild, stooping man of fifty. He was so quiet, but so sincere in his attentions. . . . He is altogether of the contemplative, theorising order.' (Charlotte, *Letter*)

(Above) Cornhill, where the premises of Messrs Smith, Elder were situated. 'We found 65 to be a large bookseller's shop, in a street almost as bustling as the Strand.' (Charlotte, *Letter*)

(Right) The Chapter Coffee House

edition from Aylott and Jones and prepared to reissue it; boxes of books came regularly from Cornhill to Haworth; correspondence between Charlotte, Smith and Williams became frequent. It seemed as if the Brontës' lives had emerged at last into the sunshine. But their hopes were again frustrated.

*Death of Branwell and Emily*

On 24 September Branwell suddenly died, of consumption. His father was broken-hearted, his sisters, too noble to welcome his departure as a relief, forgave him everything as they gazed at his marble features, from which death had erased the signs of dissipation. Emily caught cold at his funeral; consumption developed; and after an agonizing period during which she refused to see a doctor, refused to rest, insisted on performing her usual domestic duties, resented any expression of sympathy, she was torn out of life on 19 December 1848. Her superb poem, *No Coward Soul is Mine*, was stated by Charlotte to be the last she wrote. This is inaccurate, for it is dated January 1846 and other verses follow; nevertheless this poem gives an impression of Emily, her courage, her vision of life, which may properly accompany her to the grave.

> *No coward soul is mine*
> *No trembler in the world's storm-troubled sphere*
> *I see Heaven's glories shine,*
> *And Faith shines equal, arming me from Fear.*
>
> *O God within my breast*
> *Almighty, ever-present Deity!*
> *Life, that in me has rest*
> *As I, Undying Life, have power in thee!*
>
> *Vain are the thousand creeds*
> *That move men's hearts, unutterably vain,*
> *Worthless as withered weeds*
> *Or idlest froth amid the boundless main*
>
> *To waken doubt in one*
> *Holding so fast by this infinity . . .*

It has been much debated whether grief at her brother's death, or disappointment over the failure of *Wuthering Heights*, accelerated the progress of Emily's illness. Charlotte has said that the sight of Emily's unexpressed disappointment spoiled her happiness in her own success. Certainly it is peculiarly painful when two members of a family are thus set in competition.

*Death of Anne*

Scarcely was Emily in her grave before Anne showed unmistakable signs of the same disease. Considering that Anne and Emily shared a bedroom, and that hygienic precautions were in those days little understood, this was not surprising. Anne behaved with gentle docility, took all the remedies prescribed, but quickly

Scarborough in the period when Charlotte and Ellen Nussey took Anne to visit there

grew worse. In the spring of 1849 Charlotte and Ellen Nussey fulfilled a wish of Anne's to visit Scarborough. She enjoyed a glorious sunset, smiled at cliff and castle and sea, urged the boy in charge not to behave harshly to a donkey, and quietly died in the dinner-hour three days after her arrival, on 28 May 1849. She is buried in Scarborough, in St Mary's Churchyard on the cliff.

Considering that these three terrible griefs all fell upon Charlotte while she was writing *Shirley*, it is not surprising that this novel shows some defects as a work of art. There is not enough story, too much tedious dialogue, and Louis Moore, the tutor who masters and marries the rich heiress Shirley, is a failure. Charlotte hesitated much over the book's title, which reveals her uncertainty over its theme. But all the same *Shirley*, with its unusual industrial background of Luddite cloth-dressers rebelling against the installation of textile machinery, has some strong merits. The most Yorkshire, the least Celtic, of Charlotte's novels, it lacks the fire of her other works, taking place, so to speak, entirely in broad daylight.

Oakwell Hall, the Fieldhead of *Shirley*, near Birstall in Yorkshire

(Left) Interior of Oakwell Hall

(Right) Reward notice concerning the murder of a clothier in 1812. There were at least two such incidents during the Luddite rising, from which Charlotte drew the attack on Robert Moore in *Shirley*

'Calm your expectations, reader,' says Charlotte on its first page: 'Something real, cool and solid lies before you; something as unromantic as Monday morning.' Louis Moore, a variant of Charlotte's M. Heger, could not survive in this robust Yorkshire air, but all the Yorkshire characters, from the manufacturer Hiram Yorke – who could speak both dialect and elegant English, but out of true Yorkshire independence spoke the more dialect the higher the rank of the person he addressed – to cloth-dresser William Farren with his definition of 'clean pride and mucky pride', are thoroughly real and true to their county. All Charlotte's Yorkshire acquaintance are brought into use: the Taylors, the local curates and vicars, her own father; even the Anglo-Belgian Robert Moore has a touch of Mary Taylor's self-seeking brother Joe, and Hortense, though undoubtedly drawn from a Brussels schoolmistress, wears Aunt Branwell's pattens. The character of Shirley herself, 'sister of the spotted, bright, quick, fiery leopard', said to be a portrait of Emily as she might have been if rich and free, is a noble creation. English fiction had to wait a very long time before being able to welcome another heroine so intelligent and spirited. Best of all is Caroline Helstone, the ordinary girl who quietly, decently, in lonely silence, breaks her heart over her rejected love. Ellen Nussey believed Caroline to be herself, and indeed in appearance she is so; but her heartbreak is Charlotte's. A few insignificant textual errors are out-balanced by the authentic detail of the Luddite riot, gained from Mr Brontë's reminiscences of 1812.

# REWARDS.

WHEREAS, two Villains did, on the Night of Wednesday the 22nd. Day of July Instant, feloniously SHOOT at and WOUND *John Hinchliffe*, of *Upper-Thong*, in the West Riding of the County of York, Clothier, with intent to MURDER him, of which Wound he lies in a dangerous state.

## A Reward of 200 Guineas

will be given to any Person who will give such Information, as may lead to the Apprehension and Conviction of either of the said Villains.

AND WHEREAS, John Scholefield Junior, of Nether-Thong, in the said Riding, is strongly suspected of being concerned in the said Murderous attempt, AND HAS ABSCONDED.

## A Reward of Twenty Guineas

is hereby offered to any Person, who will apprehend the said John Scholefield, and lodge him in any of his Majesty's Prisons, and give Information thereof, or give such Private Information as may lead to his apprehension; *and Inviolable Secrecy will be Observed.*

The said John Scholefield is by Trade a Cloth-Dresser, about 21 Years of Age, 5 Feet 10 Inches High, Brown Hair, Dark Complexion, rather stout made: commonly wears a Dark coloured Coat, made rather short, and Lead coloured Jean Pantaloons.

The above Rewards will be paid upon such Information, Apprehension, and Conviction as above mentioned by

## Mr. John Peace, of Huddersfield,

in the said County of York, Treasurer to the Huddersfield Association.

William Makepeace Thackeray                    Samuel Rogers

*Shirley* was finished by August 1849, and the manuscript was picked up in Haworth in September by a subordinate member of Smith, Elder: the red-headed Scotsman, James Taylor. Smith, Williams and Taylor all praised the book but had some reservations similar to those felt today. *Shirley*, however, published on 26 October 1849, was well received by Press and public, though not with such acclaim as *Jane Eyre*. Charlotte received £500 for the book. She sent a copy to the 'economic' novelist Harriet Martineau, who approved it warmly; a very appreciative letter reached her from a novelist then unknown to her personally, Elizabeth Gaskell; reviews poured in; the identity of the author began to be known.

*In London*    For the next two years Charlotte's life was a strange amalgam of solitude and society. At home, the silence in the Parsonage was such that the tick of the clock could be heard all day long. In London, where the Smiths received her each year, she met Thackeray, attended some of his lectures on English Humorists, visited the National Gallery, the Zoo, the Crystal Palace, a theatrical performance, the House of Commons, an exhibition of Turner's paintings; dined with critics at George Smith's house, at Thackeray's in her own honour; breakfasted with the Poet Laureate, Samuel Rogers; met Harriet Martineau and her brother; heard

The Great Exhibition of 1851 and (below) a cartoon on the Exhibition

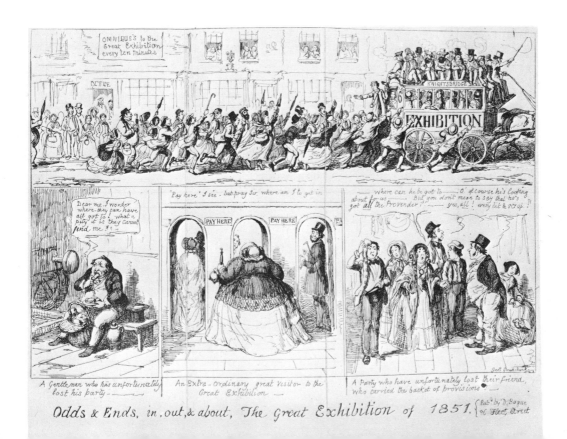

Portrait of Charlotte, by
George Richmond. This
crayon drawing was the
gift of George Smith to
Mr Brontë, on whose
death Mr Nicholls took
it to Ireland with him.
He bequeathed it to the
National Portrait Gallery

D'Aubigné, Cardinal Wiseman and F.D. Maurice preach; had her portrait painted by the fashionable George Richmond. (She never met Dickens.) It cannot be said that any of these encounters influenced her ideas or work. She was extremely shy, lacked the beauty or conversational ease which would have given her confidence in joining the badinage of the London literary world, and was apt to take utterances with Haworth literalness. Accordingly there are respectfully amused (but pathetic) anecdotes of her appearances 'in mittens, in silence, in seriousness', as Thackeray's daughter said, with her great kindling eyes and tiny body. She had, as Thackeray recognized, an indomitable honesty and independence of thought which she maintained in all its integrity – she scolded Thackeray for his cynicism, indeed, severely.

Elizabeth Cleghorn Gaskell, by George Richmond. 'She is a woman of the most genuine talent – of cheerful, pleasing and cordial manners and – I believe – of a kind and good heart.' (Charlotte, *Letter*)

A most important event occurred in 1850, namely the meeting of Charlotte and Mrs Gaskell. In March Sir James Kay-Shuttleworth, medical and educational reformer, drove over with his wife from her castellated mansion in Gawthorpe, Lancashire, to Haworth, and urged Charlotte to accept an invitation to Gawthorpe as their guest. Charlotte did not want to go, but Mr Brontë, impressed by the Shuttleworths' social standing, insisted on acceptance. The visit was a bore, but led to a further visit to the Shuttleworths in August, this time at Briery Close, their home above the shores of Lake Windermere. Mrs Gaskell arrived there that evening, and her account of the 'little lady in black silk gown', though incorrect as to some particulars of the Brontë history, is highly perceptive and illuminating. Charlotte, thin, short, undeveloped, plain, with reddish face and

Three of Mrs Gaskell's four daughters: Meta, Flossy and Marianne. Her youngest child, Julia (not shown here), born in 1846, was Charlotte's particular favourite and may have influenced her portrayal of Paulina in *Villette*

(Below) Plymouth Grove, Manchester. 'And we've got a house. Yes! . . . My dear! It's £150 a year, and I daresay we shall be ruined. We have a greenhouse at the new house – to be.' (Mrs Gaskell, *Letter*)

Sir James Kay-Shuttleworth          Lady (Janet) Kay-Shuttleworth

missing teeth and overhanging brow, but with a singularly sweet voice and very exact verbal expressions, comes vividly before us. Mrs Gaskell, the wife of a noted Unitarian preacher in Manchester, with three young daughters and a son (who died as an infant), a large establishment run by several maids, and a wide intellectual acquaintance whom she incessantly visited and received, would seem an unlikely friend for the spinster daughter of Haworth Parsonage. But Lily, as those who knew Mrs Gaskell well called her, was one of the sweetest, kindest and most intelligent of women, and a good novelist to boot – *Mary Barton* had already been published. Lily and Charlotte, though not on first-name terms, became sincere and lasting friends, an occurrence most fortunate for English literature.

Charlotte was now busy, in September 1850, writing a biographical notice of Ellis and Acton Bell to be placed in front of Smith, Elder's new edition of *Wuthering Heights* and *Agnes Grey*. She also wrote 'a few lines of remark' on *Wuthering Heights*, and a short preface to additional selections from the poems of Ellis and Acton Bell, published by Smith, Elder. While Charlotte's poems in memory of her sisters appear meagre in feeling and conventional in versification, these prose pieces are among the most moving and tragic words she ever wrote.

It is from these that we gain the deepest and clearest view of the characters of Emily and Anne, and of Charlotte's intense sorrow at their loss. She wrote thus, she said, 'because I felt it a sacred duty to wipe the dust off their gravestones and leave their dear names free from soil', and her words are worthy of this touching intention.

*George Smith*    Another event of 1850, which might otherwise have had great importance, brought no fruition, though from Charlotte's answer to Ellen Nussey's teasing in January 1851 it appears that Ellen expected consequences and Charlotte perhaps hoped for them. George Smith invited Charlotte to meet his sister and himself in Argyllshire and go on to Edinburgh, where his young brother was at school. She engaged partly in this excursion, but when a further jaunt down the Rhine was vaguely mooted, thought this unwise. Were there no vast barrier of age, fortune and so on, and men and women married whom they liked, wrote Charlotte rather wistfully . . . but other reasons regulate matrimony and she is content to have Smith as a friend. It is interesting to read what Smith replied when questioned about the matter by Mrs Humphry Ward, forty-eight years later:

Edinburgh in 1847

No, I never was in the least in love with Charlotte Brontë . . . I never was coxcomb enough to suppose that she was in love with me. But I believe that my mother was at one time rather alarmed.

Poor Charlotte! 'The idea of the "little man" shocks me less,' says she. This *James Taylor* little man is the red-haired Scotsman, James Taylor, and when he appears in Haworth in the April of 1851 it is clear that he has come to ask Charlotte's hand in marriage. But when he approached, 'my veins ran ice'. It was impossible to think of him as a husband; though Papa liked him she gave him no chance to make the proposal. Yet his departure leaves bitterness and ashes, an entire crumbling away of a prospect of hope, in fact a complete blank. Taylor goes out to India to run a branch of Smith, Elder there; he writes to Charlotte, but the letters are of a tedious travelogue kind; the affair is over.

This year, 1851, was depressing for Charlotte in other ways. Messrs Smith, Elder, naturally eager for another novel from her, yet declined to publish *The Professor*, even if refurbished, and urged her to take her time over a new novel. Charlotte began *Villette*, but, as is easy to see from the first six chapters, the story

George Smith. 'A tall young man. . . . He is a *practical* man.' (Charlotte, *Letter*)

did not march. In the autumn the lonely author fell ill with an infection of the liver; the mercury compound then usually prescribed for this did not suit Charlotte, and she suffered all the wretched side-effects which an allergy can induce. She struggled on, bitterly conscious of the absence of her sisters' advice and encouragement, but it was not until early November in the following year that the book was finished.

At last on 20 November she posted it to Smith, Elder. Of payment, £20 was to come direct to Charlotte, the rest to be invested, like her other earnings, in the Funds. She heard no word from Smith, Elder till on Saturday, 4 December, the £20 Bank Bill reached her 'in a cover without a line'. This cold and dilatory reception distressed Charlotte so much that she was preparing to rush up to Cornhill when a letter from Smith, arriving on the Sunday, relieved her anxiety. She was disappointed, however, and so probably was Mr Brontë, to find that she was to receive only £500 in all.

*Villette*      It cannot be wondered at if George Smith and W. S. Williams were startled and somewhat dismayed when they read *Villette*. Lucy Snowe's early life and trials are the reverse of exciting, while Mrs Bretton and her lively son Graham are too much like Mrs Smith and her son George for comfort, especially in the later part when Graham becomes Dr Bretton and Lucy almost loves him. Dr Bretton at

# VILLETTE.

By CURRER BELL,

AUTHOR OF "JANE EYRE," "SHIRLEY," ETC.

IN THREE VOLUMES.

VOL. I.

LONDON:
SMITH, ELDER & CO., 65, CORNHILL.
SMITH, TAYLOR & CO., BOMBAY.
———
1853.
The Author of this work reserves the right of translating it.

Title-page of first edition of
*Villette*

first prefers the frivolous Ginevra, but when that mercenary young minx elopes with a conceited colonel-count, turns to the really exquisite little character, Paulina de Bassompierre. Among other originals, Paulina may owe some traits to Mrs Gaskell's youngest daughter, Julia, who had stolen Charlotte's heart when she met her the previous year. The background of Mme Beck's boarding-school for young ladies in Villette (that is, Brussels), the striking characterizations of Mme Beck and her teacher-kinsman, M. Paul Emanuel (that is M. and Mme Heger), the piercing anguish of Lucy herself in her love and loneliness, form a superb, highly original masterpiece of art which alarmed some Victorian readers by the intensity of its emotion. Harriet Martineau, for example, whose guest in Ambleside Charlotte had happily been for a week in 1850 – where she met the Arnold family at Fox How – declared roundly that she did not like the love in *Villette*, either its kind or its degree. This, of course, was precisely its tremendous strength, and when the novel appeared in 1853 it was greeted by most of the reading public with a burst of acclamation.

Charlotte had repeatedly warned George Smith that the materials available to her for fiction were not abundant. Now that she had finally, once and for all, used her Belgian experience, pressing out its essence till there was nothing left to use, she probably felt this exhaustion, all too familiar in any case to writers at the conclusion of a creative work, with especial keenness and depression. In April of this year George Smith met at a ball a girl he fell in love with, and with his usual impetuosity married her within a few months. James Taylor was now away in India, and the parcels of books he used to supervise for loan to Charlotte were now sometimes overlooked, sometimes ill chosen, so that she proudly begged Smith, Elder not to trouble themselves further in the matter. Publishers are busy people, much engaged with the next book on their list; if an author produces nothing for a year or two they are apt to lose interest in that author. The *réclame*, the publicity about the identity of the author of *Jane Eyre* was over. Viewed from Haworth, in fact, Charlotte's prospects appeared a complete blank, and it was probably this desolation which led her to accept, though not very enthusiastically, a new venture.

*Arthur* *Nicholls*  The Rev. Arthur Bell Nicholls was an Ulsterman born of Scottish parents in County Antrim in 1818; orphaned early, he was brought up by a headmaster uncle in Banagher (County Offaly); he graduated from Trinity College, Dublin in 1844 and became curate of Haworth in the following year. Two years younger than Charlotte, he was a very serious, almost grave, reserved, religious young man of strong convictions; highly conscientious in the performance of his parish duties and narrow in his ideas. From the first Ellen Nussey guessed his inclination towards Charlotte and was ready to approve, but Charlotte could not perceive the interesting germs of goodness Ellen discerned in him; she disliked his narrowness of mind and found him tedious. She drew him as Mr Macarthy, the fourth curate in *Shirley*, making him decent, decorous and reliable, even though to be invited to tea with a Dissenter unhinged him for a week. Probably the first improvement in Charlotte's feelings towards him occurred when he roared with laughter over the *Shirley* curates and read all the scenes about them 'aloud to Papa'.

For some time Charlotte had been uneasily aware of constraint and awkwardness in Nicholls's behaviour in her presence, and when one evening in December 1852, just after the disappointing reception of *Villette* by George Smith, Nicholls on leaving Mr Brontë's study tapped on the parlour door, she guessed in a flash what was coming. But she had not realized how strong his feelings for her were. Pale, shaking from head to foot, speaking with difficulty in a low but vehement tone, Nicholls made her understand what this declaration meant to him. She asked if he had spoken to Mr Brontë; he said, he dared not. She half led, half pushed him from the room, promising him an answer on the morrow, then went immediately to her father with news of the proposal. Mr Brontë was furious.

Mary Taylor

Ellen Nussey in later life

Charlotte's own accounts of this courtship and eventual engagement, given in her letters to Ellen Nussey as it went along, could not be bettered in the finest novel in the world. Mr Brontë's jealous fury, expressing itself as snobbish resentment – a curate with £100 a year marry his famous daughter! Mr Nicholls's stubborn passion, which almost unseated his reason – he would not eat or drink; stayed shut up in his lodgings at the Browns' (though he still took poor old Flossy out for walks); broke down in the Communion Service, while the village women sobbed around; was rude to a visiting Bishop; resigned his Haworth curacy but agreed to remain till Mr Brontë found another curate; volunteered as a missionary to Australia but finally took a curacy at Kirk Smeaton, in the West Riding itself. Charlotte, exasperated by Nicholls's lack of the qualities she desired in a husband, infuriated by her father's ignoble objections to the match, conscious of the absence of alternatives. The villagers, torn between the opposing parties – some say they would like to shoot Mr Nicholls, but they give him a gold watch as a parting present. What a tragic drama – or a roaring comedy, depending on its result.

Facsimile of marriage certificate of Arthur Bell Nicholls and Charlotte Brontë

Love, coupled with Charlotte's loneliness and Mr Brontë's dissatisfaction with his new curate, Mr De Renzi, triumphed. Mr Nicholls wrote repeatedly to Charlotte. No woman dislikes being loved for herself alone, and Nicholls loved Charlotte Brontë, not Currer Bell; eventually she replied. Mr Nicholls came to stay at neighbouring Oxenhope with his friend the vicar. Charlotte and he took walks together. Presently these communications were confessed to Mr Brontë, and Charlotte admitted her desire to become better acquainted with her suitor. And so, on 11 April 1854, Charlotte wrote to Ellen:

In fact, dear Ellen, I am engaged. . . . I am still very calm, very inexpectant. What I taste of happiness is of the soberest order. I trust to love my husband – I am grateful for his tender love to me. I believe him to be an affectionate, a conscientious, a high-principled man; and if, with all this, I should yield to regrets, that fine talents, congenial tastes and thoughts are not added, it seems to me I should be most presumptuous and thankless. Providence offers me this destiny. Doubtless then it is the best for me.

This, from the creator of those great lovers Jane Eyre, Caroline Helstone and Lucy Snowe, has an almost unbearable pathos.

116

in the County of *York*

| e of Marriage. | Father's Name and Surname. | Rank or Profession of Father. |
|---|---|---|
| eaton | William Nicholls | Farmer |
| ... | Patrick Brontë | Clerk |

...urch, by ...icense by me, *Sutcliffe Sowden*

(Right) Miss Wooler in old age. She gave Charlotte away at her wedding

It was arranged that Nicholls should return to Haworth as Mr Brontë's curate, and he and his wife should live in the Parsonage with Mr Brontë. A little back room was done up in green and white to serve as his study. Mr De Renzi made as many difficulties as possible, but eventually all was settled, and the marriage was solemnized in Haworth Church on 29 June 1854, by Nicholls's friend the Rev. Sutcliffe Sowden, vicar of Hebden Bridge. To be the only guests, Miss Wooler and Ellen Nussey came to the Parsonage the night before the wedding, and this was fortunate, for after he had retired to bed Mr Brontë sent down word that he did not mean to be present at the morrow's ceremony. Who then was to 'give away' Charlotte? A hasty scrutiny of the Prayer-Book service revealed that no sex is specified for this office; accordingly Miss Wooler undertook it. Charlotte was married in a white muslin dress, with a lace mantle and white bonnet trimmed with green leaves. Although the wedding took place at eight in the morning to avoid spectators, the news leaked out into the village during the service, and several village friends came to the church door to watch the departure of the bride. The honeymoon was spent in the bridegroom's native Ireland.

It is possible to discern, and to credit, a certain alleviation in Charlotte's feelings about her marriage after her sojourn in Ireland. In Haworth, Arthur Bell Nicholls

*Marriage*

was a poor unknown curate; in Banagher he was a member of a highly respected family, whose head, Dr Bell, had been principal of a reputable boys' school in the large Cuba House. In the Bell family life everything was decorous and orderly, and it would please Mr Brontë to know that the Bells were much above the Bruntys in the social scale. A much less comfortable matter – a sudden glimpse of a very grim phantom, as Charlotte spoke of it – came into view as the honeymoon pair traversed the Gap of Dunloe in Killarney. Charlotte was thrown violently from her mount, and felt the mare kick, plunge, trample around her. She suffered no apparent injury, but one wonders if this severe shaking played some part in the plight in which Charlotte presently found herself.

It is difficult to judge whether Charlotte was happy in her marriage, or otherwise. (Probably both.) 'We've been so happy,' she murmured to her husband, and she spoke warmly of his care and affectionate company when she was ill. But to Ellen she wrote: 'It is a solemn and strange and perilous thing for a woman to become a wife.' At least she was no longer lonely, but always occupied, always needed; she had a parish and two men to care for – 'my time is not my own now' – and knew the reality of sex.

Cuba House, Banagher. Arthur Nicholls was brought up in this house, in the care of his uncle, Dr Alan Bell. Part of his honeymoon was spent here

Gap of Dunloe, Killarney. 'The guide had warned me to alight from my horse as the path was very steep – I did not feel afraid and declined – my horse seemed to go mad.' (Charlotte, *Letter*)

*Nussey Letters*

A slight skirmish took place between Arthur and Charlotte about her letters to Ellen. Arthur said they were dangerous, and required a promise that Ellen should burn them. Ellen replied with spirit that she would promise to burn if Mr Nicholls would promise not to influence their contents. Fortunately Mr Nicholls did not keep his promise – said Ellen later – so she did not keep hers.

Sir James Kay-Shuttleworth had recently built a church in Padiham (to serve Gawthorpe), and now offered the incumbency to Mr Nicholls. But Charlotte and Arthur felt bound to remain in Haworth during Mr Brontë's lifetime, since the state of his health and sight, fluctuating and uncertain for the last few years, now disabled him from conducting a parish alone. It seems to have occurred to the Nichollses that for Sutcliffe Sowden to marry Ellen Nussey and hold the incumbency of Padiham would be very agreeable. Sir James's very genuine reforms and benevolences were, however, often a little tarnished by self-interest. He wanted the husband of the famous Charlotte Brontë for his vicar, not an unknown curate; the plan fell through.

*Waterfall*

On 28 November 1854, Charlotte was just sitting down to write to Ellen when Arthur called to her to take a walk. They set off not intending to go far,

119

but presently Arthur suggested the waterfall as their destination – after the melted snow of the last few days it would be fine. The spectacle of the white torrent raving over the rocks was fine indeed, but unfortunately rain began to fall as they stood there and continued stormily as they walked the three miles home. Though Charlotte changed her soaking clothes as soon as she reached the Parsonage, she caught cold and could not throw it off.

*Illness*    She had already begun to surmise that she might be pregnant, and in January when she was attacked by sensations of nausea and faintness the possibility seemed to strengthen. A doctor was summoned and confirmed this diagnosis, declaring her present discomfort a natural effect of her condition. Charlotte suffered increasing

The Brontë Bridge and Waterfall, Haworth. 'The rugged bank and rippling brook were treasures of delight.' (Ellen Nussey, *Early Life at Haworth*)

120

sickness, ate almost nothing, became at length too weak and weary to rejoice at all in the coming of the child. Two events added to the misery of this wretched time: poor old Flossy lay quiet for a day and died in the night, and Tabby fell ill, was removed to her sister's house and died. In late January Mr Nicholls summoned Dr McTurk, the most notable Bradford physician of the period, to attend his wife; he pronounced that her illness might be long, but was not dangerous.

Charlotte, however, continued without remission her agonizing nights of sickness, her progressive emaciation, her feverish exhaustion. Presently she fell into delirium, and on the night of Saturday, 31 March 1855, she died.

*Death*

Harriet Martineau, writer of stories on economic subjects. 'Her powers of labour, of exercise and social cheerfulness are beyond my comprehension. She is a taller, larger and more strongly made woman than I had imagined.' (Charlotte, *Letter*)

Her death certificate gives *phisis* (*sic*) as the cause, which presumably is a mis-spelling for 'phthisis', pulmonary consumption such as that from which her brother and sisters perished. But modern medical opinion cites *hyperaemesis gravidarum*, i.e. excessive sickness in pregnant woman, as the cause or at least a contributory cause of her death. Whether her fall in Ireland brought about some structural lapse will never be known.

The death of the author of *Jane Eyre* inevitably produced an outburst of news-paper publicity. Tributes by Harriet Martineau and others appeared, but some of the old mistakes and *canards* concerning Charlotte were brought out afresh, and the confusion of praise and blame, truth and error, made brief correction difficult. Ellen Nussey took alarm about one particular article, and implored Mr Nicholls

THE LIFE

OF

CHARLOTTE BRONTË,

AUTHOR OF

"JANE EYRE," "SHIRLEY," "VILLETTE," &c.

BY

E. C. GASKELL,

AUTHOR OF "MARY BARTON," "RUTH," &c.

"Oh my God,
—— Thou hast knowledge, only Thou,
How dreary 'tis for women to sit still
On winter nights by solitary fires
And hear the nations praising them far off."
AURORA LEIGH.

IN TWO VOLUMES.
VOL. II.

LONDON:
SMITH, ELDER & CO., 65, CORNHILL.
1857.

[The right of Translation is reserved.]

THE

PROFESSOR:

WITH POEMS.

BY

CHARLOTTE BRONTË.

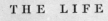

HOUSE IN DAISY LANE.

LONDON:
SMITH, ELDER AND CO., 15 WATERLOO PLACE.
1873.

Title-page of first edition of Mrs Gaskell's *Life of Charlotte Brontë* (1857)

(Right) Title-page of *The Professor* by Charlotte Brontë, in the first illustrated edition of the Brontës' works (1873)

to ask Mrs Gaskell to undertake an honourable defence of her friend. Mr Nicholls pooh-poohed this idea, but as the errors continued to appear and even grew wilder Mr Brontë began to deem it advisable that some authentic statement should be made. Accordingly he invited Mrs Gaskell to write a life of Charlotte. She agreed, carried out the task with the greatest conscientiousness, perception and charm, and produced the magnificent *Life of Charlotte Brontë*, one of the finest biographies in English literature. Her handling of awkward points in the Brontës' lives – Cowan Bridge, Branwell, Mrs Robinson, Mr Brontë himself – aroused much controversy; she did not understand the immense value of the Angria and Gondal writings; and her skilful disinfecting of the Heger letters, in Victorian times so menacing to Charlotte's reputation, is saddening and mistaken; but although much has since been added to the Brontë story as she told it, very little has had to be corrected. Her insight was prodigious. The *Life* appeared in 1857, and in the same year *The Professor* was at last published, both from Smith, Elder.

*Mrs Gaskell's Biography*

123

Haworth Parsonage and Church, as drawn by Mrs Gaskell in 1855 ▶

Martha Brown. One of the many children of the sexton, John Brown, she came as a servant to the Parsonage at the age of ten, stayed till 1861, and accompanied Mr Nicholls to Ireland after Mr Brontë's death

In 1860 the fragment of a novel, *Emma*, by Charlotte was printed in the *Cornhill* magazine with an introduction by Thackeray. This opening sketch of a plain little girl dumped by a trickster father on a genteel girls' boarding-school and abandoned without resources shows a great deal of intensity and power, and could perhaps have made another *Jane Eyre* if Charlotte had lived to improve and finish it.

Mr Nicholls remained faithfully with Mr Brontë in Haworth for the six long years which remained of the old man's life. He was a somewhat stern guardian of the bedridden invalid Mr Brontë rapidly became, and allowed himself a strong dislike of references to his wife's fame, refusing, for example. to baptize infants with the names of any of the Brontë family. Mr Brontë, learning this, once baptized an infant in his bedroom from a water-jug – a sufficient indication of the terms on which the two men stood. When Mr Brontë died in 1861 Mr Nicholls returned to Banagher, taking with him his wife's portrait, her wedding-dress (of which a copy has been made), some of Charlotte's letters and other mementoes, including Mr Brontë's dog Plato and Martha Brown. He made a happy second marriage with his cousin, but did not forget Charlotte. Forty years later, when the critic Clement Shorter prepared to write *Charlotte Brontë and Her Circle*, he found at Banagher among other cherished relics two diary notes of Emily and Anne, in a tin box, and some of the minute childhood writings wrapped in newspaper at the bottom of a drawer.

In 1872 Messrs Smith, Elder employed the artist Edmund Morison Wimperis to prepare an illustrated edition of the Brontë novels. Wimperis came to Yorkshire and was in close consultation with Ellen Nussey, so that his graceful and pleasing wood engravings represent at least Ellen's identification of the places portrayed in the novels. It is fairly certain, then, that the real places depicted contributed some elements to the Brontës' fictitious creations, but a novelist's locations are sometimes multiple in source.

Interest has not diminished, but continually increased, in the Brontës' writings. The Brontë Society was formed in 1893. Two years later a museum of relics was established in two rooms over the Yorkshire Penny Bank premises in Haworth. In 1927 Sir James Roberts, a native of Haworth who as a boy knew the Brontës, generously provided means for a new Rectory, thus acquiring the Parsonage; and in 1928 he handed over its title-deeds to the Brontë Society. Haworth Parsonage, thus become a Museum, has gradually acquired a very large number of relevant manuscripts, letters, first and foreign editions, and personal relics, and this collection has been tremendously enriched by the permanent loan in 1929 of the Brontëana of Henry H. Bonnell, a citizen of Philadelphia. These include first editions, manuscripts, letters, furniture, and above all abundant and fascinating examples of the childhood writings.

*Brontë Parsonage Museum*

Today, historical studies, biographies, fresh editions of the novels, stage, radio and television plays about the Brontës or founded on their writings, abound, and a questionnaire to librarians has shown that among nineteenth-century fiction the popularity of *Jane Eyre* and *Wuthering Heights* is second only to that of Dickens's novels.

In 1968, more than ninety-seven thousand persons from all over the world visited the Brontë Parsonage Museum.

Matthew Arnold spoke truth when in his elegy *Haworth Churchyard* he wrote of the Brontës:

> *. . . a course*
> *Short, yet redoubled by fame.*

The Churchyard at Haworth  ▶

1777 Patrick Brontë born in County Down.

1783 Maria Branwell (afterwards Mrs Brontë) born in Penzance.

1802–06 Patrick at Cambridge. Takes degree of BA.

1806–09 Patrick holds curacies in Essex, Shropshire, Yorkshire.

1811, 1813, 1815, 1818. Patrick publishes locally *Cottage Poems, The Rural Minstrel, The Cottage in the Wood, The Maid of Killarney.*

1812 Marries Maria Branwell.

1813 Maria Brontë born at Hartshead.

1815 8 February. Elizabeth Brontë born at Hartshead.

1816 21 April. Charlotte Brontë born at Thornton.

1817 26 June. Patrick Branwell Brontë born at Thornton.

1818 30 July. Emily Jane Brontë born at Thornton.

1820 17 January. Anne Brontë born at Thornton.
Patrick appointed to incumbency of Haworth.

1820 The Brontës move to Haworth Parsonage.

1821 Mrs Brontë dies.

1823 Rev. Patrick Brontë tries to remarry, but fails.
Miss Elizabeth Branwell ('Aunt') at Haworth.

1824 July. Maria and Elizabeth Brontë at Cowan Bridge Clergy Daughters' School.
Charlotte (August) and Emily (November) to Cowan Bridge School.

1825 Maria and Elizabeth leave Cowan Bridge and die.
Patrick fetches Charlotte and Elizabeth home.

1826 The four Brontë children invent imaginary worlds and write about them in tiny handwriting in tiny home-made booklets. This continues more or less all their lives.

1831 Charlotte goes to Miss Wooler's school at Roe Head. Makes friends with Ellen Nussey (who keeps her letters) and Mary Taylor.

1832 Charlotte leaves Roe Head.

1835 Emily a pupil at Roe Head.
Branwell studies painting with a Leeds artist, William Robinson.

1835-37 Branwell and Charlotte write to *Blackwood's*, Southey, Wordsworth, but receive no encouragement.

1836 Anne at Roe Head. Branwell intends to enter Royal Academy Schools in London, but does not do so. He opens a studio in Bradford and paints portraits, but is unsuccessful.

1837 Emily becomes governess at school near Halifax.

1839 Anne becomes governess with Mrs Ingham at Mirfield.
Charlotte becomes governess with Mrs Sidgwick at Stonegappe.
March. Charlotte's first proposal of marriage (Rev. Henry Nussey).
August. Charlotte's second proposal (Rev. James Bryce).

1840 Branwell becomes a tutor and then a railway clerk. He writes to Hartley Coleridge. Anne becomes governess at Thorp Green.

1841 Charlotte writes to Wordsworth and takes governess situation with the Whites at Rawdon.
Project to establish a school of their own.

1842 Charlotte and Emily go to the Heger school in Brussels.
'Aunt' dies and they return to Haworth.

1843 January. Charlotte returns to Brussels but leaves in December.
Branwell becomes tutor to Robinsons at Thorp Green.

1844 School scheme revived.

1845 Rev. A. B. Nicholls comes to Haworth.
Anne leaves Thorp Green. Branwell is dismissed. Family all at home together, with a sense of failure. Branwell drinks, does no work, gets into debt. Charlotte chances on Emily's recent poems and proposes publication of joint volume.

1846 Publication of *Poems* by Currer, Ellis and Acton Bell. The three girls are each writing a novel. Emily's

*Wuthering Heights* and Anne's *Agnes Grey* are accepted, but Charlotte's *The Professor* is refused.
Charlotte takes her father to Manchester oculist for cataract operation and begins to write *Jane Eyre*.

1847  October. *Jane Eyre* published by Smith, Elder. Immediate great success.
December. *Wuthering Heights* and *Agnes Grey* published together. Failures.

1848  July. *The Tenant of Wildfell Hall* published.
24 September. Branwell dies.
19 December. Emily dies.

1849  28 May. Anne dies.
26 October. *Shirley* published.

1850  Charlotte meets Mrs Gaskell.

1851  Charlotte's third proposal of marriage (James Taylor of Smith, Elder).

1853  28 January. *Villette* published.

1854  29 June. Charlotte marries The Rev. A. B. Nicholls.

1855  31 March. Charlotte dies.
July. Mr Brontë invites Mrs Gaskell to write an account of Charlotte's life.

1857  March. Mrs Gaskell's *Life of Charlotte Brontë* is published.
*The Professor* is published.

1861  7 June. Patrick Brontë dies.

1872  October. Publication of first illustrated edition of the Brontë works.
The artist, Edmund Morison Wimperis, consulted Ellen Nussey about the localities mentioned in the novels.

1893  Foundation of Brontë Society.

1928  Haworth Parsonage becomes Brontë Parsonage Museum.

# NOTES ON THE PICTURES

*Frontispiece* THE BRONTË SISTERS: portrait by Patrick Branwell Brontë, *c.* 1835. Infra-red photography has recently shown that the 'pillar' space in the centre was originally occupied by a male figure corresponding in appearance to Branwell. See Ingeborg Nixon in *Transactions of the Brontë Society*, part 69 (1959). *National Portrait Gallery, London.*

5 MOUNTAINS OF MOURNE. By courtesy of the Irish Tourist Board. *Photo J. Allan Cash.*

6 BIRTHPLACE of Patrick Brontë, Emdale, County Down. *Photo by courtesy of the Brontë Society of Ireland.*

JOHN WESLEY (1703–91): portrait by Nathaniel Hone RA, 1766. *National Portrait Gallery, London.*

7 PARISH CHURCH SCHOOL of Drumbally-roney, County Down. *Courtesy of the Brontë Society of Ireland.*

8 ST JOHN'S COLLEGE, Cambridge: engraving, 1819. *Courtesy of the Trustees of the British Museum.*

9 WOODHOUSE GROVE SCHOOL, Apperley Bridge, near Bradford, 1812. From *In the Footsteps of the Brontës* by E. A. Chadwick published by Sir Isaac Pitman & Sons Ltd. *Photo Tom Scott.*

10 MARIA BRANWELL aged sixteen: portrait by J. Tonkin, 1799. Her father was a merchant and town councillor. From a painting in the possession of Captain Branwell. *Courtesy of the Brontë Parsonage Museum.*

ST OSWALD'S, Guiseley Parish Church near Leeds. *Photo G. Bernard Wood.*

11 PENZANCE, CORNWALL: from *Voyage Round Great Britain* by William Daniel, 1825.

12 TITLE-PAGE of *Cottage Poems* by the Reverend Patrick Brontë. *Courtesy of the Brontë Parsonage Museum.*

TITLE-PAGE of *The Cottage in the Wood* by the Reverend Patrick Brontë. *Courtesy of the Brontë Parsonage Museum.*

13 MRS BRONTË as a young woman: anonymous portrait. *Courtesy of the Brontë Parsonage Museum.*

14 THORNTON VICARAGE, birthplace of Charlotte Brontë. Later a butcher's shop. *Courtesy of the Brontë Parsonage Museum.*

REVEREND PATRICK BRONTË as a young man: anonymous portrait, *c.* 1825. *Courtesy of the Brontë Parsonage Museum.*

THE OLD BELL CHAPEL, Thornton. *Courtesy of the Brontë Parsonage Museum.*

135

*Notes*

14 INTERIOR of the Old Bell Chapel, Thornton: anonymous painting. *Bolling Hall Museum, Bradford. Photo by kind permission of Mrs Ivy Holgate.*

15 THE PARSONAGE, Haworth, *c.* 1855. *Courtesy of the Brontë Parsonage Museum.*

16 CHURCH OF ST MICHAEL and All Saints, Haworth: before 1880. *National Buildings Record.*

OLD HAWORTH CHURCH. The aisle was widened and the galleries added in 1755. *Courtesy of the Brontë Parsonage Museum.*

17 ELIZABETH BRANWELL (?): anonymous portrait. 'A very small, antiquated little lady. She wore caps large enough for half a dozen of the present fashion, and a front of light auburn curls over her forehead. She always dressed in silk.' Ellen Nussey, *Early Life at Haworth. Courtesy of the Brontë Parsonage Museum.*

18 HAWORTH VILLAGE. *Photo Bill Brandt.*

20 HAWORTH MOOR. *Photo Edwin Smith.*

22 RAWFOLDS MILL, 1812: engraving, from *The Bookman*, October 1904.

23 HANDCROPPERS AT WORK, 1814: from *Costumes of Yorkshire* by George Walker, 1885. Textile workers who became Luddites when their hand-labour was superseded by 'frames'.

24 REVEREND CARUS WILSON: drawn on stone by J. Dickson. 'A black pillar! The straight, narrow, sable-clad shape standing erect on the rug.' Charlotte, of the Reverend Mr Brocklehurst in *Jane Eyre. Courtesy of the Brontë Parsonage Museum.*

25 COWAN BRIDGE SCHOOL: engraving by Jewitt of Derby, 1824. Charlotte was admitted on 10 August 1824. This building was used until 1833. *Courtesy of the Brontë Parsonage Museum.*

27 TUNSTALL CHURCH, near Cowan Bridge. *Photo G. Bernard Wood.*

28 SAMPLER made by Charlotte when she was twelve, completed in April 1828. *Courtesy of the Brontë Parsonage Museum.*

A PAGE from 'The History of the Year 1829' by Charlotte Brontë. *Courtesy of the Brontë Parsonage Museum.*

DOUBLE PAGE of 'The History of the Young Men' written by Charlotte, *c.* 1825. Actual size. *Courtesy of the Brontë Parsonage Museum.*

29 SKETCH by Anne Brontë, aged eight and a half. *Courtesy of the Brontë Parsonage Museum.*

'MAP of the Great Glass Town Printed and Sold by Sergeant Tree': frontispiece to 'The History of the Young Men' by Branwell Brontë. *Courtesy of the Trustees of the British Museum.*

31 'BELSHAZZAR'S FEAST': mezzotint by John Martin. *Courtesy of the Trustees of the British Museum.*

32 DUKE OF WELLINGTON: portrait by Thomas Heaphy, 1813–14. *National Portrait Gallery, London.*

33 'YOUNG MEN'S MAGAZINE', 1830: edited by Charlotte. *Courtesy of the Brontë Parsonage Museum.*

TITLE-PAGE of 'Letters from an Englishman' by Branwell Brontë. *Courtesy of the Brotherton Collection, Leeds University.*

35 ROE HEAD: drawing by Anne Brontë. 'A cheerful, roomy, country house.' Mrs Gaskell, *Life of Charlotte Brontë*, 1857. *Courtesy of the Brontë Parsonage Museum.*

36 ELLEN NUSSEY: drawing by Charlotte. 'When I first saw Ellen I did not care for her. . . . She is without romance . . . but she is good; she is true; she is faithful, and I love her.' Charlotte (Letter). *Courtesy of the Brontë Parsonage Museum.*

37 RYDINGS, Birstall. At one time the home of Ellen Nussey. From *The Bookman*, October 1904.

38 STAINED-GLASS WINDOW from the Red House, Gomersal. Described by Charlotte in *Shirley*. Now set up in the new wing of Haworth Parsonage (the Brontë Parsonage Museum). *Photo G. Bernard Wood.*

39 BREAD RIOTS: from *The Looking Glass*, 1830.

40 HAWORTH MAIN STREET. 'The flag-stones with which the steep ascent is paved are placed end-ways, in order to give a better hold to the horses' feet.' Mrs Gaskell, *Life of Charlotte Brontë*, 1857. *By permission of the Brontë Bookshop, Haworth Post Office. Photo by Photoway.*

41 OBVERSE AND REVERSE of silver medal held by Charlotte while at Roe Head, 1831–2. *Courtesy of the Brontë Parsonage Museum.*

42 AUNT BRANWELL'S TEAPOT. *Courtesy of the Brontë Parsonage Museum.*

43 TITLE-PAGE of 'The Foundling/A Tale of our own Times' by Charlotte, 1833. *By courtesy of the Trustees of the British Museum. Photo Brontë Parsonage Museum.*

44 ENTRANCE HALL, Haworth Parsonage. *Courtesy of the Brontë Parsonage Museum.*

45 BRANWELL BRONTË: plaster portrait medallion by Joseph Bentley Leyland. *Courtesy of the Brontë Parsonage Museum.*

45 REVEREND PATRICK BRONTË aged fifty-six: photograph. 'Even at this time Mr Brontë struck me as looking very venerable, with his snow-white hair. . . . His white cravat was not then so remarkable as it grew to be afterwards.' Ellen Nussey, *Charlotte's Early Life at Haworth. Photo Walter Scott.*

46 THE PARLOUR, Haworth Parsonage, to-day. The furniture is contemporary, but not all actually owned by the Brontës. *Courtesy of the Brontë Parsonage Museum.*

47 EMILY BRONTË: portrait by Branwell Brontë, *c.* 1835. *National Portrait Gallery, London.*

ANNE BRONTË: portrait by Charlotte. *Courtesy of the Brontë Parsonage Museum.*

48 SIR WALTER SCOTT (1771–1832): portrait by J. G. Gilbert, 1867. *National Portrait Gallery, London.*

49 'THE GUN GROUP': portrait of Anne, Charlotte, Branwell and Emily (left to right), by Branwell.

50 IMAGINARY PORTRAIT from Charlotte's sketchbook. Probably an Angrian character. *Courtesy of the Brontë Parsonage Museum.*

51 ROBERT SOUTHEY, 1845: marble portrait bust by J. G. Lough. *National Portrait Gallery, London.*

52 DIARY FRAGMENT written by Emily, 26 June 1837. Size $5\frac{3}{8}$ by $4\frac{3}{8}$ inches. Sketch shows Anne and Emily at the table. *Courtesy of the Brontë Parsonage Museum.*

53 SHIBDEN VALLEY, where some of the scenes of *Wuthering Heights* are perhaps set. *Photo G. Bernard Wood.*

54 SHIBDEN HALL, near Halifax, south entrance. The relative situations of Shibden Hall in the valley and High Sunderland on the moor correspond to that of Thrushcross Grange and Wuthering Heights. Both houses are within walking distance of Law Hill. *Photo G. Bernard Wood.*

55 WATH CHURCH, near Ripon, where Charlotte visited with the Sidgwick family when governess at Gateshead Hall, Stonegappe. This is the church in which Jane Eyre and Rochester were to have been married. *Courtesy of the Brontë Parsonage Museum.*

56 SKIPTON, entrance to the Castle: engraving by Stowe after Whittock, 1829. *Victoria and Albert Museum.*

57 SEA BATHING at Bridlington, 1814: from *Costumes of Yorkshire* by George Walker, 1885.

ANNE'S DOG FLOSSIE, by Charlotte Brontë. *Courtesy of the Brontë Parsonage Museum.*

58 KEIGHLEY, old station: engraving, *c.* 1847. *Photo by courtesy of the 'Keighley News'.*

59 AUTOGRAPH manuscript of a poem by Emily Brontë. *Courtesy of the Brontë Parsonage Museum.*

60 WILLIAM ROBINSON (1799–1839): self-portrait. *Leeds City Art Galleries.*

61 LECTURE on sculpture by Sir Richard Westmacott at the Royal Academy, Somerset House, 1830. The Royal Academy moved to Trafalgar Square in 1836. *Guildhall Museum.*

TOM SPRING'S PARLOUR at the Castle Tavern, Holborn, where Branwell is said to have spent his time in London: from *Pierce Egan's Book of Sports,* 1832.

62 PLEDGE of the Haworth Temperance Society signed by Rev. Patrick Brontë as President and by Branwell as one of the secretaries. *Courtesy of the Brontë Parsonage Museum.*

63 THE BLACK BULL HOTEL, Haworth, and the Church gates and stocks in their original positions. *By permission of the Brontë Bookshop, Haworth Post Office. Photo by Photoway.*

64 MRS KIRBY: painting by Branwell. *Courtesy of the Brontë Parsonage Museum.*

65 BRADFORD from the south-east: from *The History of Bradford* by John James, 1841.

JOSEPH BENTLEY LEYLAND (1811–51): photograph. *Reproduced by kind permission of Miss Mary Leyland.*

66 JOHN BROWN: portrait by Branwell Brontë. *Courtesy of the Brontë Parsonage Museum.*

HARTLEY COLERIDGE: portrait by Robert Tyson, painted before 1846. *University of Texas.*

67 KEEPER, Emily's dog: watercolour by Emily Brontë, 24 April 1838. At Emily's funeral he 'walked alongside of the mourners, and into the church, and stayed quietly there all the time that the burial service was being read. When he came home, he lay down at Emily's

chamber door, and howled pitifully for many days.' Mrs Gaskell, *Life of Charlotte Brontë*, 1857. *Courtesy of the Brontë Parsonage Museum.*

FIRST PAGE of a letter to Ellen Nussey from Charlotte Brontë, 1840. *Bonnell Collection, no. 165. Courtesy of the Brontë Parsonage Museum.*

HERO, a moorland Merlin hawk which Emily Brontë had as a pet: watercolour by Emily, 27 October 1841. *Courtesy of the Brontë Parsonage Museum.*

68 SOWERBY BRIDGE drawn on stone by A. F. Tait: from *Views on the Manchester and Leeds Railway*, 1845.

69 LORD NELSON INN, Luddenden. 'I would rather give my hand than undergo again . . . the malignant yet cold debauchery . . . which too often marked my conduct there.' Branwell Brontë (Letter). *Photo G. Bernard Wood.*

71 CHARTISTS marching in procession, London, 1842. *Guildhall Museum.*

73 THE HEGER FAMILY: portrait by Ange François, 1847. *By kind permission of Monsieur René Pechère, Brussels.*

74 PROSPECTUS for the Pensionnat Heger. *Courtesy of the Brontë Parsonage Museum.*

75 HÔTEL DE VILLE, Brussels: engraving by Samuel Prout. *Victoria and Albert Museum.*

76 THE PENSIONNAT HEGER, Brussels: photograph. *Courtesy of the Brontë Parsonage Museum.*

77 CONSTANTIN HEGER in middle life: anonymous portrait. *By kind permission of Monsieur René Pechère, Brussels.*

78 THE PENSIONNAT HEGER and garden from the rear: photograph. *Courtesy of the Brontë Parsonage Museum.*

79 MADAME HEGER in 1886: photograph. *Courtesy of the Brontë Parsonage Museum.*

MONSIEUR HEGER in 1886: photograph. *Courtesy of the Brontë Parsonage Museum.*

80 ONE OF CHARLOTTE BRONTË'S LETTERS to Monsieur Heger, 8 January 1845. *Courtesy of the Trustees of the British Museum.*

81 HAWORTH PARSONAGE. *Photo Bill Brandt.*

82 PROSPECTUS of the proposed Brontë school, 1884. *Courtesy of the Brontë Parsonage Museum.*

83 BIRTHDAY NOTE written by Emily Brontë, 30 July 1845. *Courtesy of the Brontë Parsonage Museum.*

85 'There shines the moon, at noon of night': beginning of a Gondal poem written by Emily Brontë, March 1837 and copied into the manuscript reproduced here in February 1844. *Courtesy of the Trustees of the British Museum.*

86 REVEREND ARTHUR BELL NICHOLLS: photograph. *Courtesy of the Brontë Parsonage Museum.*

87 TITLE-PAGE of *Poems* by Currer, Ellis and Acton Bell, 1846. *Courtesy of the Brontë Parsonage Museum.*

88, 89 HIGH WITHENS, Haworth Moor. *Photo Yorkshire Post Newspapers Ltd.*

90 HIGH SUNDERLAND, Halifax. 'A quantity of grotesque carving lavished over the front . . . a wilderness of crumbling griffins and shameless little boys.' Emily Brontë, *Wuthering Heights*. *Photo G. Bernard Wood.*

91 PONDEN HALL, near Haworth. *Photo G. Bernard Wood.*

92 FIRST PAGE of the autograph manuscript of *Jane Eyre* by Charlotte Brontë, 16 March 1847. *Courtesy of the Trustees of the Brontë Parsonage Museum.*

94 NORTON CONYERS, near Ripon. *Photo G. Bernard Wood.*

TUDOR roundabout fireplace, Wycoller Hall, Wycoller, Lancs. *Photo G. Bernard Wood.*

95 THE 'MADWOMAN'S' ROOM, Norton Conyers. *Photo G. Bernard Wood.*

OAK STAIRCASE, Norton Conyers. Charlotte Brontë must have ascended this staircase to reach the traditional 'madwoman's' room. *Photo G. Bernard Wood.*

96 TITLE-PAGE of *Jane Eyre*, 1847. *Photo by courtesy of the Brontë Parsonage Museum.*

97 TITLE-PAGE of *Wuthering Heights*, 1847. *Photo by courtesy of the Brontë Parsonage Museum.*

TITLE-PAGE of *The Tenant of Wildfell Hall*, 1848. *Photo by courtesy of the Brontë Parsonage Museum.*

98 W. S. WILLIAMS: photograph. 'A pale, mild, stooping man of fifty. He was so quiet, but so sincere in his attentions. . . . He is altogether of the contemplative, theorising order.' Charlotte (Letter). *Courtesy of the Brontë Parsonage Museum.*

99 CORNHILL, London: engraving. *Guildhall Museum.*

THE CHAPTER COFFEE HOUSE: from *Drawings of Old London*, by Philip Norman, FSA. *Victoria and Albert Museum.*

101 THE NEW SPA and Saloon, Scarborough: lithographed by H. B. Carter, 1839. *Courtesy of Scarborough Art Gallery.*

102 OAKWELL HALL, Birstall. The Fieldhead of *Shirley*. *Photo G. Bernard Wood.*

THE GREAT HALL, Oakwell Hall. *Photo G. Bernard Wood.*

103 REWARD NOTICE, Luddite rising, 1812. Batley Museum. *Photo by courtesy of the Tolson Memorial Museum, Huddersfield.*

104 W. M. THACKERAY (1811–63): portrait by F. Stone, *c.* 1839. *National Portrait Gallery, London.*

SAMUEL ROGERS (1763–1863): portrait by T. Phillips. *National Portrait Gallery, London*

105 INTERIOR of the Great Exhibition: from the transept looking east, 1851. *Guildhall Museum.*

'ODDS AND ENDS in and out and about the Great Exhibition': drawing by George Cruickshank from *The Adventures of Mrs Sandboys*, by Henry Mayhew, 1851.

106 CHARLOTTE BRONTË: portrait by G. Richmond, 1850. This crayon drawing was the gift of George Smith to Mr Brontë, on whose death Mr Nicholls took it to Ireland with him. He bequeathed it to the National Portrait Gallery. *National Portrait Gallery, London.*

107 MRS GASKELL: portrait by G. Richmond, 1851. 'She is a woman of the most genuine talent – of cheerful, pleasing and cordial manners and – I believe – of a kind and good heart!' Charlotte (Letter). *National Portrait Gallery, London.*

108 META, FLOSSY AND MARIANNE GASKELL: drawing by A. C. Duval, 1845. *Reproduced by kind permission of Mrs Margaret Trevor Jones. Photo Stanley Travers.*

108 MRS GASKELL'S HOUSE, 84 Plymouth Grove, Manchester. 'And we've got a house. Yes! . . . My dear! It's £150 a year, and I daresay we shall be ruined. We have a greenhouse at the new house–to be.' Mrs Gaskell (Letter). *Photo Manchester Public Libraries.*

109 SIR JAMES KAY-SHUTTLEWORTH. Doctor, medical and educational reformer, Secretary of the Committee of the Council of Education, created baronet in 1849. He took the name of Shuttleworth on his marriage to the Shuttleworth heiress. '. . . a man of polished manners with clear intellect and highly polished mind. . . . Frank he is not, but on the contrary – politic.' Charlotte (Letter). *Private Collection.*

JANET, LADY KAY-SHUTTLEWORTH (1817–72): portrait by Sir Francis Grant, PRA. '. . . a little woman thirty-two years old with a pretty, smooth, lively face . . . grace, dignity, fine feelings were not in the inventory of her qualities.' Charlotte (Letter). *Private Collection.*

110– EDINBURGH from Calton Hill: from *A*
111 *Complete View of the City and Environs*, by T. Stuart, 1847.

112 GEORGE SMITH: engraved portrait. *Courtesy of the Brontë Parsonage Museum.*

113 TITLE-PAGE of *Villette*, 1853. *Photo by courtesy of the Brontë Parsonage Museum.*

115 MARY TAYLOR. *Courtesy of the Brontë Parsonage Museum.*

ELLEN NUSSEY in later life. *Courtesy of the Brontë Parsonage Museum.*

116 MARRIAGE CERTIFICATE of Arthur Bell Nicholls and Charlotte Brontë: facsimile in the Brontë Parsonage Museum. *By permission of the Brontë Bookshop, Haworth Post Office. Photo by Photoway.*

117 MISS WOOLER in old age: from *The Bookman*, October 1904.

118 CUBA HOUSE, Banagher. *Courtesy of the Brontë Society of Ireland.*

119 GAP OF DUNLOE: from *The Lakes of Killarney*, 1857.

120 THE BRONTË BRIDGE, Sladen Valley, near Haworth. *Photo G. Bernard Wood.*

122 HARRIET MARTINEAU (1802–76): portrait by R. Evans, 1834. 'Her powers of labour, of exercise and social cheerfulness are beyond my comprehension. She is a taller, larger and more strongly made woman than I had imagined.' Charlotte (Letter). *National Portrait Gallery, London.*

123 TITLE-PAGE of the first edition of Mrs Gaskell's *Life of Charlotte Brontë*, 1857.

TITLE-PAGE of *The Professor*, volume IV of *Life and Works of Charlotte Brontë and her sisters*, 1873. This was the first illustrated edition of the works of the Brontës. Illustrated by E. M. Wimperis.

124– HAWORTH CHURCH and Parsonage: draw-
125 ing by Mrs Gaskell, 1855. From *Life of Charlotte Brontë*, by Mrs Gaskell, 1857. *Photo by courtesy of the Brontë Parsonage Museum.*

126 MARTHA BROWN, died 19 January 1880. *Courtesy of the Brontë Parsonage Museum.*

128 HAWORTH CHURCHYARD. *Photo Bill Brandt.*

We acknowledge the co-operation of Winifred Gérin, FRSI, in obtaining photographs for the illustrations on pages 65, 66 and 108.

# INDEX

*Page numbers in italics refer to illustrations*

Since Charlotte, Emily, Anne and Branwell Brontë appear throughout this book, their names are not indexed

142